THE LIBRARY
ST. MARY'S COLLEGE OF M[...]
ST. MARY'S CITY, MARYLAND 20686

PLAYS OF PROTEST

THE NATUREWOMAN
THE MACHINE
THE SECOND-STORY MAN
PRINCE HAGEN

BY

UPTON SINCLAIR

NEW YORK
MITCHELL KENNERLEY
MCMXII

Republished, 1970
Scholarly Press, 22929 Industrial Drive East
St. Clair Shores, Michigan 48080

*Copyright 1911 by
Mitchell Kennerley*

Library of Congress Catalog Card Number: 75-115275
Standard Book Number 403-00293-1

This edition is printed on a high-quality,
acid-free paper that meets specifications
requirements for fine book paper referred
to as "300-year" paper

PLAYS OF PROTEST

The Naturewoman
The Machine
The Second-Story Man
Prince Hagen

CONTENTS

The Naturewoman	3
The Machine	73
The Second-Story Man	141
Prince Hagen	157

PREFACE

Of the plays here offered, the first in order of writing was "Prince Hagen": a dramatization of a novel published nearly ten years ago. The author had always been dissatisfied with this novel, and he found that a new version of the theme was taking shape in his mind. The play which resulted was tried out under the author's direction at the Valencia Theatre, San Francisco, in January, 1909. In the light of the experience thus gained the play was entirely rewritten, and the new version of it is here presented.

The second of the plays in point of time was "The Second-story Man." This little sketch, with two others, was given by a dramatic company, organized by the writer, in a dozen or so cities of California in 1909. The playlet is perhaps the most dramatic thing the author has written; concerning the opening performance the San Francisco *Bulletin* declared that "the applause was the most tumultuous ever witnessed in any theatre in this city"; and in two other cities the audience compelled the repetition of the piece. As an illustration of the difficulties encountered by a writer who seeks to use the stage in America as a medium for the setting forth of radical ideas, it may be mentioned that the production was offered to the head of the vaudeville "syndicate" in San Francisco, who declared his unqualified approval of it; but upon an account of the play being telegraphed to New

York, word came in reply that nothing so radical could be accepted. "The Second-story Man" has been since presented in vaudeville on several occasions, but always with the same result—enthusiastic acceptance by the audience, and inability to obtain regular bookings from those "higher up." The playlet has been published, and also presented under Socialistic auspices, in England and Australia, in Germany, France and Italy.

The third play to be written was "The Machine," concerning which the following explanation should be made. Four or five years ago the writer set to work upon what he intended to be a trilogy of novels portraying the life of the city of New York. The first of these novels, "The Metropolis," dealt with what calls itself "society"; the second, "The Moneychangers," with "high finance"; the third, which was to be called "The Machine," was to carry its hero through a political career, presenting a study of "Tammany Hall" and the slums. This work was undertaken at a time when the writer was in wretched health and under great nervous strain. He was unable to make either of the two published volumes what he had intended; and the third volume he was unable to write at all—the most superficial study of the material brought him into contact with so much misery and oppression that he found the attempt was literally wrecking him.

The theme, however, kept haunting him, and conditions which he had discovered cried out for publicity. He found that the work was taking, in his mind, the shape of a play, and so finally it came to be written. He is aware of the fact that two inadequate novels and a play constitute a somewhat dubious literary form. However, "The Machine" is to be read by itself—he makes the explanation here merely in order that readers of "The Metropolis" and "The Moneychangers" may understand why they find the same characters in the play, and may know what

PREFACE

was the story to which the two novels were intended to lead up.

When this play was finished I took it to a manager-friend. He said, "It is as good as any political play that I ever saw, but the public won't stand for that kind of political play." I then took it to another friend, one of the most successful playwrights in America, a man who has made a large fortune out of plays which portray modern conditions. I told him that I had written a drama dealing with politics and high finance in New York.

He said, "I will read it, but I know in advance that it will be impossible."

"Why?" I asked.

"You have treated it realistically, have you not?"

I hesitated for a moment, then answered, "Yes."

"Of course," he said, "and the public won't stand for realistic treatment of such a theme. If you want to deal with politics and high finance, you must treat it sentimentally, you must 'fake' it, as I did in '———.'" He named one of the most successful of his plays.

After which I took the play to a third friend, an actor-manager who ranks at the top of his profession. He said, "I read it with interest, but I couldn't put on a play like that. Tammany Hall would close me up in a week."

I narrate these anecdotes by way of illustrating what a man encounters who attempts to found a revolutionary drama in America. I can only assure my readers that I intend to stand by my guns. I do not intend to deal with American capitalism "sentimentally," I do not intend to "fake" my portrayal of it. I spent ten years of my life fighting for the privilege of writing my novels as I wished them. I am willing to spend another ten years fighting for the privilege of writing plays. I believe that in "The Machine" I have produced an acting play, which the people of New York will some day see on the stage. They will see it, if for no other reason than because they need to know the facts which it sets forth.

The youngest of my dramatic children is "The Naturewoman"; and she is too young to have had much of a past. Those to whom I showed her were unanimous in the opinion that I would have to put some more clothes upon her before she could be admitted upon the New York stage. A friend sent her to that "specialist in immoral and heretical plays," Mr. George Bernard Shaw, who made the comment: "Of course, plenty of dramatic and literary faculty has gone to the making of it, but Sinclair is a traitor to civilization, and his main thesis, which is that a woman with the habits and ideas of a porpoise is superior to a woman with the habits and ideas of Madame Roland, will not wash." My reply to this is, that "The Naturewoman" represents a definite reaction in my attitude to life. For the first fifteen years of my independent intellectual existence, I was a disciple of the ideal of "spirituality"; I sought the things of the mind and "soul" exclusively—until suddenly I awakened to a realization of the fact that I had lost the power of digesting food. Now I have come to the conviction that it is better to have "the habits and ideas of a porpoise"—with a porpoise's digestion—than it is to have "the habits and ideas of Madame Roland"—plus the headaches and backaches which most of the Madame Rolands of my knowledge are obliged to contend with.

In conclusion, I desire to put on record the fact concerning "Prince Hagen" and "The Machine," that they were offered to the New Theatre, and declined. Referring to the former play, the representative of the institution remarked to my play-agent that it was "a powerful work, but contrary to the principles of the founders." This phrase has stayed in my mind; I am tempted to take it up and immortalize it. It would be by no means an uninstructive performance to take the list of the twenty founders of the New Theatre, as printed upon all its programs, and study their careers, both public and private, and inquire as to the "principles" which have actuated them. The New Theatre was founded to improve dramatic taste in this country, to lead the way to a new dramatic awakening. So far, in the judgment of many critics, it has failed; and it is surely worth while that some one who is free to speak plainly should point out the reason for the failure.

It is the obvious fact that the next task before the American people is to take their political and industrial affairs out of the hands of gentlemen of the type of the founders of the New Theatre; and that the rousing of the American people to this task is the duty now before the country's writers and thinkers. In every nation of Europe to-day there is a school of dramatists who are enlisted more or less consciously and definitely in such an undertaking. Hauptmann, Halbe, Gorki, Andreiev, Heijermans, Van Eeden, Maeterlinck, Brieux, Hervieux, Bernard Shaw, Granville Barker, John Galsworthy—these men are the creators of worth-while and vital drama; and that we can name no such men in America means simply that in America the drama has not yet come to face the realities of modern life. It will not be long, I think, before we shall witness a change in this regard. The point I am making here is, that the New Theatre can have nothing to do with any such awakening—at least not so long as its "founders" have any control whatever over its destinies.

Of what service these present plays may prove in the work of establishing a revolutionary drama in this country, the writer will make no attempt to predict. Only this much he will say—that they are the work of a man who has faced the realities of modern life; who is a passionate lover of the theatre, and intends to devote the greater part of his time from now on to the attempt to write for it. It is his plan to print his plays in book-form, and leave it for those to whom they may appeal to find some way of getting them before the public.

THE NATUREWOMAN

CHARACTERS

OCEANA: the Naturewoman.
M. SOPHRONIA MASTERSON: of Beacon Street, Boston.
QUINCY MASTERSON, M.D.: her husband.
FREDDY MASTERSON: her son.
ETHEL MASTERSON: her younger daughter.
MRS. LETITIA SELDEN: her elder daughter.
HENRY SELDEN: Letitia's husband.
REMSON: a butler.

ACT I

Drawing-room of the Masterson home; afternoon in winter.

ACT II

The same; the next afternoon.

ACT III

A portion of the parlor, as a stage; the same evening.

ACT IV

Henry Selden's camp in the White Mountains; afternoon, a week later.

THE NATUREWOMAN

ACT I

Scene shows a luxuriously furnished drawing-room. Double doors, centre, opening to hall and stairway. Grand piano at right, fireplace next to it, with large easy-chair in front. Centre table; windows left. and chairs.

At rise: ETHEL *standing by table; a beautiful but rather frail girl of sixteen; opening a package containing photograph in frame.*

ETHEL. Oceana! Oceana! [*She gazes at it in rapture.*] Oh, I wonder if she'll be as good as she is beautiful! She must be! Oceana! [*To* REMSON, *an old, white-haired family servant, who enters with flowers in vase.*] No message from my brother yet?

REMSON. Nothing, Miss Ethel.

ETHEL. Look at this, Remson.

REMSON. [*Takes photograph.*] Is that your cousin, Miss Ethel?

ETHEL. That's she. Isn't she lovely?

REMSON. Yes, miss. Is that the way they dress in those parts?

ETHEL. The natives don't even wear that much, Remson.

REMSON. It must be right warm there, I fancy.

ETHEL. Oh, yes . . . they never know what cold weather is.

REMSON. What is the name of it, Miss Ethel?

ETHEL. Maukuri—it's in the South Seas.

REMSON. It seems like I've heard of cannibals in those parts, somewhere.

ETHEL. Yes, in some of the groups. But this is just one little island by itself . . . nothing else for a hundred miles and more.

REMSON. And she's lived there all this time, Miss Ethel?

ETHEL. Fifteen years, Remson.

REMSON. And no folks at all there?

ETHEL. Not since her father died.

REMSON. [*Shakes his head.*] Humph! She'd ought to be glad to get home, Miss Ethel.

ETHEL. She didn't seem to feel that way. [*Takes book and seats herself by fireplace.*] But we'll try to make her change her mind. Just think of it . . . she's been forty-six days on the steamer!

REMSON. Can it be possible, miss?

ETHEL. Wasn't that the street door just now, Remson?

REMSON. I thought so, Miss Ethel. [*Moves to door.*] Oh! Mrs. Masterson.

MRS. MASTERSON. [*In doorway; a Boston Brahman, aged fifty, wearing street costume, black.*] Any news yet, Remson?

REMSON. None, madam.

MRS. MASTERSON. Master Frederick is at the dock?

REMSON. Yes, madam.

DR. MASTERSON. [*Enters; slightly younger than his wife, a dapper little man, bald and henpecked.*] No news from the steamer, my dear?

MRS. MASTERSON. None.

REMSON. Anything further, madam?

MRS. MASTERSON. Nothing.

Exit REMSON.

ACT I] THE NATUREWOMAN

DR. MASTERSON. It'll be too bad if Oceana has to spend this evening on the steamer.

MRS. MASTERSON. Have you taken to calling her by that ridiculous name also?

DR. MASTERSON. Surely she has a right to select her name!

MRS. MASTERSON. I was present when she was christened; and so were you, Quincy. For *me* she will remain Anna Talbot until the day she dies.

DR. MASTERSON. Anna or Oceana . . . there's not much difference, it seems. [*Takes paper and sits by window; they do not see* ETHEL.] Weren't Letitia and Henry to be here?

MRS. MASTERSON. Letitia was . . . but she's never on time. There's the bell now. [*Looks at photograph.*] Humph! So Ethel's had it framed! I declare . . . people ought not to be shown a photograph like that . . . it's not decent.

DR. MASTERSON. My dear! It's the South Sea Islands!

MRS. MASTERSON. [*Severely.*] *This* is Back Bay. Oh! Letitia!

LETITIA. [*Enters; aged about twenty-eight, prim and decorous, patterned after her mother; black street costume, with furs.*] No news from the steamer, it seems! Dear me, such weather!

MRS. MASTERSON. You didn't walk, I hope?

LETITIA. No, but even getting into the stores! I'm exhausted.

DR. MASTERSON. [*Looking from paper.*] Henry coming?

LETITIA. He said he might drop in. He's curious to see the lady.

DR. MASTERSON. Humph! No doubt!

LETITIA. Mother, I wish you'd try to do something

with Henry. He's so restless and discontented . . . he's getting to be simply impossible.

MRS. MASTERSON. I'm going to talk to him to-day, my dear.

LETITIA. Fancy my going out and burying myself in the country! And he means it . . . he's at me all the time about it!

MRS. MASTERSON. Well, don't go, my dear!

LETITIA. Don't worry yourself . . . I've not the least intention of going. Such things as we modern women have to endure! Only fancy, he's got an idea he wants to be where he can work with his hands!

MRS. MASTERSON. Henry ought to have discovered these yearnings before he married one of the Mastersons. As my daughter, you have certain social obligations to fill . . . your friends have a claim upon you, quite as much as your husband.

LETITIA. He says he wants to take the bungalow and make it over . . . wants to plan it and work at it himself. And with me and the children sitting out on the mountain-top in the snow until he finishes, I suppose!

MRS. MASTERSON. Quincy, do you know anything about this whim of Henry's for a day-laborer's life?

DR. MASTERSON. My dear, Henry's a big, active man, and he wants something to do.

MRS. MASTERSON. But hasn't he his business?

DR. MASTERSON. I dare say there are things more thrilling to a man than commercial law-cases. And Henry's been thinking for himself . . . he says the law's a cheat.

MRS. MASTERSON. Yes, I know . . . I've heard all that. And here we are, just at this critical moment, when the girl is coming, and when he ought to be advising us about that will.

DR. MASTERSON. It seems to me, my dear, you've managed to choose your course without his aid. [*A pause.*]

I hope we shan't have to get into any quarrel with Oceana.

MRS. MASTERSON. We shall not if *I* can help it, Quincy.

LETITIA. We simply intend to be firm, father.

MRS. MASTERSON. We intend to make it clear that we are going to stand by our legal rights. With no hard feelings for her personally . . .

ETHEL. [*Rising from chair.*] Mother!

MRS. MASTERSON. Ethel!

ETHEL. Mother, this has gone just as far as it can go! I've felt all along that something like this was preparing.

MRS. MASTERSON. My dear . . .

ETHEL. Mother, this concerns me as much as it concerns any one of you. And I tell you, you have simply got to let me know about that will.

MRS. MASTERSON. My dear . . .

ETHEL. Do I understand that it is your intention to threaten to go to law, unless Oceana gives us a part of grandfather's property?

MRS. MASTERSON. Ethel, I refuse . . .

DR. MASTERSON. You might as well tell the child, Sophronia. It's perfectly certain, Ethel, that your grandfather was not of sound mind when he made the will.

ETHEL. It's perfectly certain that he hated you and mother and Aunt Letitia and me and Freddy . . . every one of us; and that he had hated us for years and years; and that he left his money to Oceana to spite us all.

MRS. MASTERSON. That's precisely it, Ethel . . .

ETHEL. And I, for one, knowing that he hated me, don't want his money. And what is more, I refuse to touch his money.

DR. MASTERSON. Not being of age, my dear, you can't . . .

ETHEL. I am near enough of age to possess my self-respect. And I shall refuse to touch one penny.

DR. MASTERSON. My child, there are a good many pennies in a half million dollars.

MRS. MASTERSON. And when you are of age, Ethel, you'll appreciate . . .

ETHEL. I shall be of age two years from now, and then I shall return to Oceana every penny of grandfather's money that may have been gotten for me.

LETITIA. Ethel!

MRS. MASTERSON. It seems to me this is a strange way for a young girl to be speaking to her parents!

ETHEL. I can't help it, mother. I am meek and patient . . . I try to let you have your way with me in everything. But this is a matter of principle, and I can't let myself be sat on.

MRS. MASTERSON. Sat on! Is that your view of your mother's attitude towards you?

ETHEL. You know, perfectly well, mother, that it's impossible for anybody to preserve any individuality in contact with you . . . that as a matter of fact, neither father nor Letitia nor Freddy nor myself have preserved a shred of it. Grandfather said that to you himself, the last time you ever saw him . . . I know it, for I've heard father say it a hundred times.

DR. MASTERSON. Well!

MRS. MASTERSON. It seems to me there's more than a trace of individuality in this present outburst, Ethel.

ETHEL. Yes, but it's the first time, mother.

LETITIA. Some one is coming. [*Turns to door.*] Oh! Henry!

HENRY. [*Enters; a handsome, powerfully-built man; smooth shaven, immaculate, reserved in manner.*] Well, has the sea-witch arrived?

MRS. MASTERSON. Not yet.

DR. MASTERSON. Freddy's gone to meet her with the limousine.

HENRY. I see. And the steamer?

MRS. MASTERSON. It was to have docked two hours ago.

HENRY. Well, that means that I won't see her till to-morrow evening. I've got to run down to Providence to-night.

LETITIA. What's the matter?

HENRY. Nothing important . . . just a business matter that requires my presence. Make my apologies; and good-bye, my dear.

    Kisses LETITIA.

LETITIA. Henry, I wish you'd wait a moment.

HENRY. What for, my dear?

LETITIA. Mother has something to say . . .

MRS. MASTERSON. I want to talk to you about this idea of going to the country in the winter-time.

HENRY. Oh! There's no use talking about that, Mrs. Masterson. I see I can't have my way, so there's no more to be said. I'm not the sort of man to sulk.

MRS. MASTERSON. But such an idea, Henry! For a delicate woman like Letitia . . .

HENRY. I know . . . I know. I'd have taken care of her . . . but that doesn't interest her. And, of course, I can't take the children away from her, and there's not much fun in the country alone. So what's the use? I give up . . . as I give up everything. Good-bye, all.

    Exit.

LETITIA. I declare—such a trial! A husband who's lost his interest in life!

MRS. MASTERSON. It's that new cook of yours, Letitia.

LETITIA. Every cook is worse.

MRS. MASTERSON. What he needs is some liver-pills. Quincy, you should attend to it! [*Rises.*] Well, I'm going upstairs. You'll stay to dinner, Letitia?

LETITIA. Yes, I want to lie down for a while.

DR. MASTERSON. And I'll beat myself a game of billiards.

Exit with LETITIA *and* MRS. MASTERSON.

ETHEL. [*Drops her book to floor, springs up and paces the room.*] Oh! If only I might change places with Oceana! If I could get away to some South Sea island, and be my own mistress and live my own life. [*Takes photograph.*] Oceana! I'm wild to see you! I want to see you dancing. Your Sunrise Dance . . . and to your own music! [*Begins to hum the Sunrise Dance.*] Oceana! Oceana!

A step in the hall, she turns.

FREDDY. [*Enters briskly; a college boy, about twenty-one, overgrown, narrow-chested, good-natured and slangy.*] Ethel!

ETHEL. [*Starts.*] Freddy! Where's Oceana?

FREDDY. She won't get here till morning.

ETHEL. Oh, Freddy!

FREDDY. They can't dock the steamer to-night . . . there's some tangle at the pier.

ETHEL. Did you go and see?

FREDDY. I telephoned about it. I didn't want to wait in this blizzard.

ETHEL. I'm so sorry!

FREDDY. Me, too. But there's no help for it.

ETHEL. So long as she doesn't miss to-morrow night! Did I read you what she said about that, Freddy? [*Takes letter from pocket.*] "I'll pray for fair weather, so that I may get there to see the beautiful dancing. There is nothing in all the world that I love more . . . my whole being seems to flow into the dance. I send you the music of my Sunrise Dance, that father composed for me. You can learn it, and I'll do it for you. I don't know, of course; but father used to think that I was wonderful in it . . . and he had known all the great dancers in Europe. It was the last thing I heard him play, before he went out in the boat, and I saw him perish before my eyes." Don't you think that she writes beautifully, Freddy?

FREDDY. Yes; it's surprising.

ETHEL. Oh, yes. Her father was an extraordinary man, Henry says . . . a musician and a poet. They had books and everything, apparently. You'd think she's been living in Europe.

FREDDY. I see.

ETHEL. Listen to this: [*Reads.*] "About my name . . . I forgot to explain. You see, Anna sounds like England . . . or New England . . . and I am not the least like those places. Father used to see me, as a little tot, diving through the breakers, and floating out in the sea, with the snow-white frigate-birds flashing by overhead; and he said I was the very spirit of the island and the wild, lonely ocean. So he called me Oceana, and that's the name I've always borne."

FREDDY. It just fits my idea of her.

ETHEL. She goes on: "You mustn't be surprised at what I am. You may think it's dreadful . . . even wicked. But at least don't expect anything like you've ever known before. Fifteen years with only cocoa-palms and naked savages . . . the Boston varnish rubs off one. But I'm going to try to behave. I expect to feel quite at home . . . I have pictures of all of you, and a picture of the house . . . I even have father's keys, to let myself in with!"

FREDDY. Can you play her music, Ethel?

ETHEL. Play it? I could play it in my sleep. [*Opens piano.*] The Sunrise Dance! [*She sits and plays.*] Listen!

> *She plunges into the ecstatic part of the music.* FREDDY *leans by the piano, watching her; she plays, more and more enthralled. The door opens softly.*

OCEANA *enters; a girl of twenty-two, superbly formed, dark-skinned, a picture of glowing health. She is clad in a short skirt and a rough sailor's reefer with cap to match; underneath this a knitted garment, tight-fitting and soft—no corsets. She carries two extremely heavy suitcases, and with no apparent effort. She sets these down and stands listening to the music, completely absorbed in it. There is the faintest suggestion of the Sunrise Dance in her attitude.*

OCEANA *is trusting, and yet with power of reserve. Throughout the action, however vehemently she speaks, she seldom really grows angry; she does not take the game seriously enough. On the other hand her enjoyment, however keen, never becomes boisterous. Her actions proceed from a continual overflow of animal health. She is like a little child, in that she cannot remain physically still for very long at a time; she moves about the room like an animal in a cage. Her speech proceeds from an overwhelming interest in the truth, regardless of all personality. She never conceals anything, and she never represses anything.*

ETHEL. [*Finishes the music, then turns, and leaps up.*] Oceana!

FREDDY. [*Turns.*] Oceana!

OCEANA. Ethel! [*Embraces her.*] Oh, my dear! How glad I am to see you!

ETHEL. Oceana! But how did you get here?

OCEANA. I came on the steamer.

FREDDY. But it isn't docked!

OCEANA. They took us to another dock.

ETHEL. [*Holds her at arm's length.*] Oh, how fine you are!

OCEANA. And you—you can play my father's music! I'm so glad!

ETHEL. You liked the way I played it?

OCEANA. I liked it! And so I know I shall like you! And I'm so happy about it—I wanted to like you!

ETHEL. But how big you are!

OCEANA. [*Laughing.*] Oh, that's the clothes. I got them in Rio. They're queer, I guess, but I only had a couple of hours. And this is Freddy! [*They shake hands.*] It's so good to be here!

FREDDY. How did you get from the dock?

OCEANA. I walked.

ETHEL. Walked all the way?

OCEANA. Of course . . . I enjoyed it.

ETHEL. But in the storm!

OCEANA. I didn't mind that. It's all new to me, you see. My dear, think of it . . . I've never seen snow before. I was fairly crazy.

She pulls off the coat and throws it on one of the suitcases.

ETHEL. I must tell mother. And Letitia! [*Opens door and calls.*] Mother! Letitia! Oceana's here!

FREDDY. [*Stoops to pick up the suitcases.*] Why . . .

OCEANA. What is it?

FREDDY. [*He moves them against the wall with a great effort.*] You don't mean you *carried* those!

OCEANA. Why, yes.

FREDDY. From the docks?

OCEANA. [*Laughs.*] Oh, dear me! I didn't mind that.

FREDDY. Well . . . I'll be blowed!

He has fallen head over heels in love with her, and whenever he is in her presence he follows her about with his eyes, like one bewitched.

OCEANA. You aren't strong as you ought to be! You stay too much in the house!

ETHEL. Here's mother!

OCEANA. Aunt Sophronia!

MRS. MASTERSON. [*Enters.*] My dear Anna! [*Kisses her upon the cheek.*] I am delighted to see you safe.

ETHEL. And Letitia!

OCEANA. Cousin Letitia!

LETITIA. [*Enters.*] My dear cousin! So glad you are here!

OCEANA. [*Looking from one to the other, as they eye her critically.*] Oh, are you really glad to see me? You must be, you know . . . for I've come so far. And you've no idea how homesick I've been.

MRS. MASTERSON. Homesick, my dear? For that wild place you left?

OCEANA. But Aunt Sophronia, that's my home! And it's God's own dream of beauty!

MRS. MASTERSON. Yes, my dear . . . I dare say . . .

OCEANA. Ah, you've never been there, or you wouldn't feel that way! Picture it as it is at this moment . . . the broad white beach . . . the sun setting and the clouds aflame . . . the great green breakers rolling in . . . the frigate-birds calling . . . the palm trees rustling in the wind! And you don't have to wrap yourself up in clothes . . . you don't have to shut yourself up in houses! You plunge through the surf, you dance upon the beach . . . naked . . .

MRS. MASTERSON. [*Aghast.*] My dear girl!

OCEANA. Oh, oh! That's so! I beg your pardon!

MRS. MASTERSON. [*Coldly.*] It will take you a little while to get used to civilized ways . . .

OCEANA. Oh, no, no, no! I know about that . . . I know how it is. Father told me about Boston.

MRS. MASTERSON. My dear . . .

OCEANA. Don't worry about me. I'm really going to try to behave myself . . . in every way. I want to get the right sort of clothes, you know. I couldn't get them on my trip . . .

MRS. MASTERSON. It's just as well, my dear. You'd best have us attend to that. You will need mourning for quite a while, you understand.

OCEANA. Mourning!

MRS. MASTERSON. Yes . . . for your grandfather.

OCEANA. But, my dear Aunt Sophronia, I couldn't possibly wear mourning! No, no! I couldn't do that!

MRS. MASTERSON. [*Astonished.*] Why not?

OCEANA. In the first place, I never mourn.

MRS. MASTERSON. But your own grandfather, my dear!

OCEANA. But I never knew him. Aunt Sophronia . . . I never saw him in my life!

MRS. MASTERSON. Even so, my dear! Hasn't he left you all his fortune?

OCEANA. But am I supposed to mourn over that? Why, I'd naturally be happy about that!

LETITIA. Oceana!

OCEANA. But surely . . . wouldn't you be happy about it?

MRS. MASTERSON. My child, one is not supposed to set so much store by mere money . . .

OCEANA. But Aunt Sophronia, money is power! And isn't anybody glad to have power? What else did I come here for?

MRS. MASTERSON. I had hoped you had come home for some other things . . . to see your relatives, for instance.

ETHEL. Here's father!

OCEANA. Uncle Quincy!

DR. MASTERSON. [*Enters.*] My dear girl! You have come! [*Embraces her.*] Why, what a picture you are! A very storm from the tropics! My dear Oceana!

OCEANA. I'm so glad to get here.

DR. MASTERSON. Yes, indeed! I can believe it! And

a strange experience it must have been . . . your first plunge into civilization!

OCEANA. Yes, Uncle Quincy! It's been horrible!

DR. MASTERSON. Horrible, my dear? In what way?

OCEANA. It's been almost too much for me. Really . . . I could understand how it might feel to be sick!

DR. MASTERSON. Why, what did you see?

OCEANA. Everything! It rushed over me, all at once! The people . . . their dreadful faces! And such noises and odors and sights!

DR. MASTERSON. I hadn't realized . . .

OCEANA. And then the saloons! Rows and rows of them! It is ghastly!

LETITIA. My dear cousin, mother and I contribute regularly to a temperance society.

OCEANA. But that hasn't helped, has it? I'm almost wild about such things—they were the real reason I came home, you know.

MRS. MASTERSON. How do you mean?

OCEANA. They had got to my island! They are turning it into a hell!

DR. MASTERSON. In what way?

OCEANA. Why, it's a long story. I didn't write . . . it would have taken too long. Two years ago there was a ship laid up . . . and the crew found, quite by accident, that our island rock is all phosphate; something very valuable . . . for fertilizer, it seems. So they bought land from the natives, and now there's a company, and a trading-post, and all that. And oh, my people are going all to pieces!

MRS. MASTERSON. The natives, you mean?

OCEANA. Yes . . . the people I have loved all my life. And I've tried so hard . . . I've pleaded with them, I've wept and prayed with them! But they're lost!

LETITIA. You mean rum?

OCEANA. I mean everything. Rum, and cocaine, and sugar, and canned food, and clothes, and missionaries . . . all civilization! And worse yet, Aunt Sophronia . . . ah, I can't bear to think of it!

MRS. MASTERSON. What?

OCEANA. You wouldn't let me tell you what. [*In a low voice.*] Imagine my people, my beautiful people, with the soft, brown skins and the big black eyes, and hair like the curtains of night. They are not savages, you understand . . . they are gentle and kindly. They ride the rushing breakers in their frail canoes, they fish and gather fruits in the forests, they dream in the soft, warm sunshine . . . they are happy, they are care-free, their whole life is a song. And they are trusting, hospitable . . . the wonderful white strangers come, and they take them into their homes, and open their hearts to them. And the strangers go away and leave them a ghastly disease, that rages like a fire in their palm-thatched cabins, that sweeps through their villages like a tornado. And the women's hair falls out . . . they wither up . . . they're old hags in a year or two. And the babies . . . I've helped bring them into the world . . . and they had no lips . . . their noses were gone! They were idiots . . . blind . . .

MRS. MASTERSON. [*Wildly.*] Anna Talbot! I must beg you to have a little discretion!

LETITIA. Why should we hear about these things, Oceana?

OCEANA. My dear, it comes from America. The ships came from here! There was one of them I saw . . . "The Mary Jane, of Boston, Mass."

MRS. MASTERSON. No doubt, among such low men . . . men of vile life . . . sailors . . .

OCEANA. No, Aunt Sophronia . . . you're mistaken! It's everywhere. Isn't it, Uncle Quincy? You're a doctor . . . *you* must know!

OCEANA. But Aunt Sophronia! You know you were!
MRS. MASTERSON. [*Sputters.*] Oh! *Oh!*
OCEANA. You were thinking to yourself, this girl's been playing around on the beaches with savages . . . and what's been happening to her?
DR. MASTERSON. My dear niece, I'm afraid you'll have to take some account of our civilized prejudices. We simply don't say everything that we think.
OCEANA. [*Springing up.*] Oh, dear me! I'm so sorry! I didn't mean to make you unhappy! I was going to be so good. I was going to try to conform to everything. Why, just think of it, Aunt Sophronia . . . in Rio I actually bought a pair of corsets. And I tried to wear them. I . . . Oceana! Around my waist! Think of it! [*She looks for sympathy.*] I couldn't stand them . . . I climbed to the topmast and threw them to the sharks. But now it seems that you all wear corsets on your minds and souls. [*A pause.*] Never mind . . . let's talk about something else. I'm getting restless. You see . . . I'm not used to being in a room . . . it seems like a box to me . . . I can hardly breathe. The air in here is dreadful . . . hadn't any of you noticed? [*Silence. Apparently nobody had.*] Would you mind if I opened a window?
MRS. MASTERSON. It is storming outside, Anna.
OCEANA. Yes, but one can exercise and keep warm Just a minute . . . please. [*She flings up a window; a gale blows in.*] Ah, feel that!

    MRS. MASTERSON, LETITIA *and* DR. MASTERSON *draw away from the window.*

MRS. MASTERSON. This is simply outrageous'
LETITIA. It is beyond all words!
DR. MASTERSON. My dear, consider
MRS. MASTERSON. I won't have that creature in my house a minute longer.

DR. MASTERSON. My dear, be reasonable!

LETITIA. *Reasonable?*

DR. MASTERSON. Consider what is at stake!

MRS. MASTERSON. But what hope have we to get anything out of such a woman?

DR. MASTERSON. We have some hope, I'm sure. If we . . .

MRS. MASTERSON. Didn't you hear her say she'd come home for nothing but the money?

DR. MASTERSON. Yes . . . but at least she's honest enough to say it, Sophronia. And she's here as our guest . . . she wants to be friendly . . . don't let it come to an open break with her!

LETITIA. But how can we *help* it, father?

DR. MASTERSON. It's just a matter of letting her talk. And what harm will that do us?

MRS. MASTERSON. But we can't lock her up in the house. And can we introduce her to our friends? To-morrow night, for instance!

DR. MASTERSON. We must manage it somehow. When we've once had an understanding with her, it won't take long to get the papers signed, and after that we won't care. Control yourself, Sophronia, I implore you! Don't let your prejudices ruin us!

ETHEL. [*Steals to them, in agitation.*] Mother, can't you be good to her? You don't understand her at all.

MRS. MASTERSON. [*Coldly.*] Thank you, Ethel . . .

ETHEL. [*To* FREDDY, *who joins them.*] Can't you say something to them, Freddy? They treat her so badly.

FREDDY. They hate her, Ethel! They couldn't understand her.

OCEANA *takes deep breaths, expelling them in short, sharp puffs.*

LETITIA. What in the world are you doing?

OCEANA. That's one of the Yogi exercises. Haven't any of you studied the Vedantas?

LETITIA. We are all Episcopalians here, Oceana.

OCEANA. Oh, I see!

She takes a deep breath and then pounds her chest like a gorilla.

MRS. MASTERSON. And pray, what is *that?*

OCEANA. I'm just getting some of the civilization out of my lungs.

A furious gale blows.

MRS. MASTERSON. Really, my dear, we shall have to leave the room. We'll all catch our death of cold.

OCEANA. My dear Aunt Sophronia, nobody ever caught a cold from winter air. Colds come from over-eating and bad ventilation. [*She closes the window.*] However, there you are! [*Eagerly.*] Now, let's have something beautiful—so that I can forget my blunders. Let's have some music. Will you play for me, Cousin Letitia?

LETITIA. I don't play, my dear.

OCEANA. What? Why, father told me you played all the time!

LETITIA. That was before my marriage.

OCEANA. Oh, I see! [*Laughs.*] The music has accomplished its purpose! [*Stops. alarmed.*] Oh! I've done it again! [*Goes to* LETITIA.] My dear cousin, believe me, I meant no offense. I'm never personal. I was simply formulating a principle of sociology!

MRS. MASTERSON. You have strange ways, my dear niece.

DR. MASTERSON. Are you always so direct, so ruthless?

OCEANA. That's the word, isn't it? That's what father taught me. Never to think about personalities . . . to go after the truth! He used to quote that saying of Nietzsche's: "To hunger after knowledge as the lion for his food!"

MRS. MASTERSON. Oh, you read Nietzsche, do you? How could you get such books?

OCEANA. We had a government steamer from New Zealand three times a year, you know. That brought our mail.

MRS. MASTERSON. And your father permitted you to read these improper things?

OCEANA. My father taught me to face the facts of my being. My father was a fighter, you know.

MRS. MASTERSON. [*Grimly.*] Yes, I knew that.

OCEANA. Life had hurt him. Some day you must tell me about it . . what it was that happened to him here in Boston. He never would talk about it, but I've often wondered. It must have been my mother. What did she do to him before she died? [*She pauses, expecting an answer.*] Was it that she was just conventional like you? [*She pauses again.*] It must have been something dreadful . . . he felt so keenly about it. He burned it into my very soul . . . his fear of civilization. And here I am . . . right in the midst of it . . . I'm letting it get its claws into me! I'm wearing its clothes . . . [*She tears at them.*] I'm breathing its air! I don't believe I can stand it! [*She paces the room restlessly.*] My soul is suffocating, as well as my body. I must have something to remind me of the sky, and the open sea, and the great spaces. I must go back again to my home, to my island! [*Stretches out her arms to them appealingly.*] Ah, can't some of you understand about it? Can't some of you take pity on me? It's so strange to me . . . so different from everything I've been used to! Aunt Sophronia!

MRS. MASTERSON. [*Takes a step reluctantly.*] My dear!

ETHEL. [*Springing forward.*] No! No! They don't understand! They don't really care.

MRS. MASTERSON. Ethel!

OCEANA. But you! Ethel!

ACT I] THE NATUREWOMAN 23

ETHEL. [*Rushes and flings herself at* OCEANA'S *feet, clutching her dress.*] Take me with you! Take me away to your island!

OCEANA. [*Turning to* FREDDY.] And you . . . won't you be my friend?

FREDDY. [*Goes to her.*] I will! [*She holds out her hand to him; he hesitates, gazing at her awe-stricken.*] May I . . . may I take your hand?

OCEANA. Why certainly!

FREDDY. [*With fervor.*] Oceana!

CURTAIN

ACT II

Scene: Same as Act I.

At rise: DR. MASTERSON *in easy-chair near the window; opens newspaper, sighs, wipes glasses, prepares to read.*

MRS. MASTERSON. [*Enters with* LETITIA.] Well!

DR. MASTERSON. Home, are you?

MRS. MASTERSON. Yes! And such a day!

LETITIA. Shopping with Oceana!

DR. MASTERSON. Humph!

MRS. MASTERSON. Imagine buying clothes for a woman who won't squeeze her waist, and won't let her skirts touch the ground!

DR. MASTERSON. Why didn't you take her to the men's department?

LETITIA. Don't make a joke of it, father.

DR. MASTERSON. How did you make out?

MRS. MASTERSON. Well, we've got her so the police won't molest her

LETITIA. We told Madame Clarice her trunks had been misplaced in the steamer hold.

DR. MASTERSON. Ingenious!

MRS. MASTERSON. Yes! Only she spoiled it all by telling the truth!

DR. MASTERSON. Where is she now?

MRS. MASTERSON. She's walking . . . she says she must have exercise.

LETITIA. The air in the limousine is close, it seems.

DR. MASTERSON. You got something she could wear to-night?

MRS. MASTERSON. Oh, yes, that part's all right. If I could only have selected the things she's going to *say* to-night!

A pause.

DR. MASTERSON. Well, and what are the signs?

MRS. MASTERSON. I don't know. I can't read her at all.

DR. MASTERSON. You haven't broached the subject yet?

MRS. MASTERSON. Not definitely. I've hinted at it. I said we were worried about the future of Freddy and Ethel.

DR. MASTERSON. And what did she say to that?

MRS. MASTERSON. She said that she'd take care of them, if I'd let her.

DR. MASTERSON. Why . . . that's promising.

MRS. MASTERSON. So I thought . . . till I found she meant taking them off to the South Seas!

DR. MASTERSON. Oh!

MRS. MASTERSON. I thought I'd wait till to-night . . . after the dancing. You see, she'll have met some company, and I thought she might be feeling more . . . more genial.

DR. MASTERSON. I understand. A good idea.

LETITIA. Miss Pilkington ought to put her in a good mood.

MRS. MASTERSON. She's passionately fond of fancy dancing, it seems. And Ethel's been writing her about to-night, so she's quite excited about it.

DR. MASTERSON. I see.

LETITIA. People are wildly jealous of us because we got Miss Pilkington to come here. Everybody's talking about it.

MRS. MASTERSON. You haven't heard any criticisms, I hope?

LETITIA. Nothing that amounts to anything.

MRS. MASTERSON. I wish I could feel comfortable about it. It seems so very daring. It's been only seven months since the funeral. To be sure . . . father and I hadn't spoken for ten years.

DR. MASTERSON. And everybody knows the entertainment is for charity.

LETITIA. And we've only asked the very best people.

DR. MASTERSON. And the date was arranged over a year ago.

LETITIA. And it isn't as if we were going to dance ourselves, mother. And then they are "Biblical Dances," too.

MRS. MASTERSON. I know—I know. But then, the world is so quick to gossip. They might say we were doing it because he left his fortune to a girl in the Cannibal Islands!

DR. MASTERSON. Perhaps it's just as well the girl's to be here.

MRS. MASTERSON. Yes, if we can keep her within bounds. I shall be on pins and needles till it's over.

LETITIA. Such a white elephant in one's home!

MRS. MASTERSON. And then the way Freddy and Ethel are behaving!

LETITIA. Freddy wanted to stay from college and Ethel from her music lesson—both of them to go and sit around in the stores while Oceana bought clothes!

DR. MASTERSON. Well, of all things!

MRS. MASTERSON. I hardly know Ethel any more!

LETITIA. And Freddy sits around and stares at her like a man out of his wits!

MRS. MASTERSON. That'll be the next thing, I suppose . . . she'll run off and marry him!

DR. MASTERSON. Well, mightn't that be a good way to solve the problem? To keep the money in the family?

MRS. MASTERSON. Quincy!
LETITIA. Besides—she mightn't marry him.
MRS. MASTERSON. Letitia!
LETITIA. Why not, mother?
MRS. MASTERSON. I'm sure, my child, you have no reason for saying anything like *that*.
LETITIA. I don't trust the minx!
   A pause.
DR. MASTERSON. Has Henry got home?
LETITIA. He's probably there now.
MRS. MASTERSON. Is he coming here to dinner?
LETITIA. I'm not sure.
MRS. MASTERSON. You'd better take my advice and not let him.
LETITIA. Why not?
MRS. MASTERSON. Because, the first thing you know, we'll have Henry in love with her, too.
LETITIA. [*Horrified.*] Mother!
MRS. MASTERSON. I mean it, my dear—quite seriously. What's the meaning of all this discontent of Henry's? I know him well enough . . . he's just the man to be taken in by the tricks of such a woman! *She'd* give him plenty of outdoor exercise! *She'd* go live in the country with him!
LETITIA. [*Springing up.*] Mother! How horrible!
MRS. MASTERSON. Forewarned is forearmed, Letitia. You listen to me, and let Henry see just as little of Anna Talbot as you can. And when he's with her, you be there, too.
LETITIA. [*In great agitation.*] I'll go home right now and see to him!
   Exit.
DR. MASTERSON. [*Sighs.*] Oh, dear! And I was waiting for Henry to play billiards with!

MRS. MASTERSON. You might get Anna to play billiards with you. No doubt she's an expert.

Exit right.

DR. MASTERSON *sighs, shakes his head, and resumes reading.*

OCEANA. [*Enters, radiant, clad in an ermine cloak.*] Well, Uncle Quincy!

DR. MASTERSON. Oceana! Bless me! How gorgeous!

OCEANA. [*Takes it off and throws it on the chair.*] It's really too warm for walking.

DR. MASTERSON. I should have thought, coming from a tropical climate . . .

OCEANA. Ah, but my blood circulates, you see. [*Sits opposite him.*] Uncle Quincy, I want to have a talk with you.

DR. MASTERSON. Yes, my dear?

OCEANA. Uncle Quincy, why do you let Aunt Sophronia and Letitia frighten you the way they do?

DR. MASTERSON. My dear girl!

OCEANA. Take yesterday afternoon, for instance—what I said about syphilis. You know I was right, and yet you didn't dare say so.

DR. MASTERSON. Really, Oceana . . .

OCEANA. You are an educated man—a man of science. You know what modern ideas are. And yet you consent to be walked all over!

DR. MASTERSON. My dear . .

OCEANA. Here are these women . . . they have leisure and opportunity . . . they ought to be doing some good in the world. And yet they haven't an idea except to act as other people think they ought to act!

DR. MASTERSON. Dear me! Dear me!

Rises and begins to pace the room.

OCEANA. Don't run away from me.

DR. MASTERSON. I'm not running away. But you are so disconcerting, Oceana . . .

OCEANA. I know; but that's only because you know that what I say is true, and you don't like to feel that anybody else knows it.

FREDDY. [*Off.*] Oceana!

OCEANA. Freddy!

FREDDY. [*Enters.*] Oh! Father's here!

OCEANA. Yes; we were having a chat.

FREDDY. [*Hesitates.*] Father, will you excuse me, please . . . I have something very important to say to Oceana. I've been waiting for her.

DR. MASTERSON. Why . . . what . . .

FREDDY. Don't ask me, please. I must have a talk with her right away. Please come, Oceana.

OCEANA. All right.

DR. MASTERSON. I was going to the billiard-room, anyway. Pray excuse me.

Exit centre.

OCEANA. [*Smiles.*] See him run! Well, Freddy, what is it?

FREDDY. [*Intensely.*] Oceana!

OCEANA. What's the matter?

FREDDY. You mustn't stay here!

OCEANA. Why not?

FREDDY. They'll ruin you, Oceana! They'll crush you, they'll spoil you forever! You must go away!

OCEANA. Why, my dear boy, how can they hurt me?

FREDDY. They will, they will! I've been thinking about it all day! I didn't go to college . . . I spent the whole day pacing the streets.

OCEANA. Why, Freddy!

FREDDY. And I want you to come away! Come away with me! I want you . . . [*Wildly.*] . . . I want you to marry me!

OCEANA. [*Aghast.*] Why, Freddy!

FREDDY. Oh, I know it's a fool way . . . to blurt it out at you like that. I thought up a hundred ways to say it to you. I had a fine speech all by heart, but I can't remember a word of it. When I see you I can't even think straight. I'm simply beside myself . . . I can't rest, I can't sleep, I can't do anything. I used to laugh at such ideas, but now I'm frightened at myself. Can't you understand me, Oceana? Oceana . . . I love you!

OCEANA. [*Whispers.*] My poor boy!

FREDDY. I don't ask you to say yes . . . I just ask you to give me a chance . . . a hope. If I thought I might win you, I'd do anything . . . anything! I'd wait for you . . . I'd work for you . . . I'd worship you! Oceana! [*He stops.*] May I . . . May I take your hand? [*She does not give it.*] Ah, no! I have no right! Oceana, listen to me! I have thought that I was in love before . . . but it was just childish, it was nothing like this. This has been a revelation to me . . . it makes all the world seem different to me. And just see how suddenly it's come . . . why, yesterday I was a boy! Yesterday I thought some things were interesting . . . and to-day I wonder how I could have cared about them. Nothing seems the same to me. And it all happened at once, it was like an explosion . . . the first instant I laid eyes on you I knew that you were the one woman I could ever love. And I said to myself, she will laugh at you.

He hesitates.

OCEANA. No, I won't laugh at you.

FREDDY. I tried to keep it to myself, but I couldn't . . . not if I were to be hanged for it. I'm just . . . just torn out of myself. I'm trembling with delight, and then I'm plunged into despair, and then I stop to think and I'm terrified. For I don't know what I can do. Everything in my life is gone—I won't know how to live if you send me away.

OCEANA. [*Gravely.*] Freddy, come sit down here. Be rational now.

FREDDY. Yes.

He sits watching her, in a kind of daze.

OCEANA. In the first place, Freddy . . . you must understand, it isn't the first time this has happened to me.

FREDDY. No, I suppose not.

OCEANA. The officers of the ships always used to fall in love with me. There were three on this last steamer.

FREDDY. Yes.

OCEANA. You say to marry you. But it's difficult for me to imagine myself marrying any man, no matter how much I loved him. One has to make so many promises, you know.

FREDDY. How do you mean?

OCEANA. You have to "love, honor and obey."

FREDDY. But, Oceana! That's a mere form.

OCEANA. No, no. It's written in the laws. All kinds of things . . . people don't realize it.

FREDDY. But surely . . . if you love a man . . . a decent man . . .

OCEANA. No decent man ought to ask a woman to sign away her self-respect.

FREDDY. [*Bewildered.*] But then . . . then . . . what would you do?

OCEANA. [*Watches him, then laughs to herself.*] Boston is such a funny place!

FREDDY. Hey?

OCEANA. Let us leave marriage out now . . . let us talk of love. Realize how much more serious it is to a woman than it is to a man. A man meets a woman and he finds her beautiful, and his blood begins to boil, and he says: "I adore you." And so she gives herself to him; and then, the next morning, he goes off and forgets all about it.

FREDDY. No, no!

OCEANA. I don't say you, Freddy. But it's happened that way. The woman, though . . . she doesn't forget. She carries a reminder. And it's not only that she has the burden of the child . . . the anguish of the birth . . . the task of suckling and rearing it. It's that she has a miniature of the man with her all the rest of her days. She has his soul there . . . blended with the thing she loves most of all in the world. And so, don't you see how careful she has to be, how desperately important the thing is to her? [*She sits lost in thought.*] I have never been in love, Freddy, not the least little bit. I have never felt that call in my blood. But some day I shall feel it; and when I do, I shall take that man as if before a court of judgment. I shall take him away with me. I shall ask myself not merely, "Is he beautiful and strong of body?" but, "Is he beautiful and strong in soul?" I would not ask that he be learned . . . he might not chance to be a cultured man. But he would be a man of power, he would be a man who could rule himself, he would be a soul without base alloy. And when I had satisfied myself as to that, I would have found my mate. I would say to him, "I wish you to be the father of my child." [*She sits again, brooding.*] I would not exact pledges of him. I would say to him, "I do not ask you to take care of me; I do not ask you to take care of my child. You may go away when you wish . . . that rests with you; but *I* wish the child." [*She pauses.*] Do you see?

FREDDY. Yes, I see. [*He gazes at her, frightened.*] And you . . . you do not feel that way about me?

OCEANA. Not the least little bit, Freddy.

FREDDY. And if I waited ever so long?

OCEANA. I do not believe that I should ever **feel it,**

[*She puts her hand upon his arm.*] My dear, dear boy! Learn to look at it as I do. Face it like a man. It is one of those things that we cannot help . . . that we do not even understand. It is the chemistry of sex; it is Nature's voice speaking to us. It means no disgrace to you that I do not love you . . . it means no inferiority, no defeat. It is the signal that Nature gives us, that we wait for, and dare not disregard. You dare not ask me to disregard it! [*He is gazing into her eyes like one entranced.*] You must let me teach you . . . you must let me help you. You must not let this mean misery and despair. Take hold of yourself. Perhaps you and Ethel can go back with me to my island . . . for I think that I am going. [*He continues to gaze at her, speechless with admiration. She presses his arm.*] Now promise me.

FREDDY. What?

OCEANA. That you will be a man.

They gaze into each other's eyes.

ETHEL. [*Off.*] Oceana!

OCEANA. Here is your sister. Let us not trouble her. [*Aloud.*] Ethel!

ETHEL. [*Enters in street costume.*] Oh, here you are! And your new clothes!

OCEANA. Do you like me?

ETHEL. No, they don't belong to you!

OCEANA. [*Laughs.*] Well, I shan't wear them long.

ETHEL. What are you going to do?

OCEANA. I'm going to design some for myself.

ETHEL. What kind?

OCEANA. I don't know yet. But it'll be something that will leave my legs outside.

ETHEL. And did you get something beautiful for tonight?

OCEANA. I got something that will do.

ETHEL. Oceana, when am I to see the dance?

OCEANA. I told you, when I have my costume.
ETHEL. But when will that be?
OCEANA. When my trunks have come.
FREDDY. They came this afternoon.
OCEANA. Oh! Then we'll have it to-morrow morning! And I'll show you my beautiful bridal-robe.
FREDDY. Bridal-robe?
OCEANA. Yes. Didn't I tell you? It was made for me by one of our King's sons. His name was Paukopi . . . that means, in our language, "Child of the Sea Foam." And he was in love with me.
ETHEL. Oh!
OCEANA. He was very sad and went away by himself. But he was a man . . . he did not go to pieces. [*She looks at* FREDDY.] He went into the forest and spent his time hunting wild birds; and he gathered their feathers and made them into this gorgeous robe . . . purple and gold and green and scarlet. He brought it and laid it at my feet, and said that it was my bridal-robe, that I must wear it at my feast.
ETHEL. Oh, how lovely!
FREDDY. [*Rises and turns away in despair.*] Oh!
ETHEL. Tell me a little about the Sunrise Dance.
OCEANA. It represents the worship of Nature. It portrays an awakening from slumber . . . you know the soft part of the music at the beginning . . .
ETHEL. Yes.
OCEANA. Then gradually I rise to my feet and gaze towards the light. There is the sun shining upon the waves of the sea, and upon the palm branches. All life is awakening and singing for joy . . . and so the music rises to an ecstasy.
ETHEL. And do you dance other things?
OCEANA. Oh, yes—lots of things.
ETHEL. Oh, Oceana! I'm just wild to see you!

ACT II]   THE NATUREWOMAN   35

OCEANA. And I'm wild to dance. I must have some vent pretty soon. You see, at home I was out of doors all the time. I hunted and fished, I swam and dived, I danced on the beach. And here . . . why, I walk down the street, and I daren't even so much as sing out loud. I have to remember that I'm a young lady, and have an ermine cloak on! Truly, I don't see how you ever stand it!

ETHEL. We were brought up that way.

OCEANA. Yes; and that's why you're undeveloped and frail. But tell me, don't you ever have an impulse to play? That beautiful snow out there—don't you want to tumble round in it and pelt each other with snowballs?

FREDDY. We did that when we were children.

OCEANA. Yes, that's the way. But I, you see . . . I'm a child still; and I expect to be always.

ETHEL. And are you always happy, Oceana?

OCEANA. Always.

ETHEL. You never . . . you never even start to feel sad?

OCEANA. Why yes, now and then. But I don't permit such moods. You see, I have the conviction that there is nothing beautiful or right about sorrow—never, under any circumstances.

ETHEL. You mean you would not mourn, even if some one you loved were to die?

OCEANA. I mean that I *did* not. [*She pauses.*] Yes, exactly . . . my father. He had been my life's companion, and they brought him home drowned; and yet I did not mourn.

ETHEL. Oceana!

OCEANA. I had trained myself . . . for just that. We had made ourselves what you might call soul-exercises; little ceremonies to remind ourselves of things we wished to hold by. The Sunrise Dance was one of those. And then, on the last day of each month, at sunset, we would sit and watch the shadows fade, and contemplate death. [*She pauses, gravely.*] We would say to ourselves that we, too, were shadows . . . rainbows in the sea-mist; that we held our life as a gift . . . we carried it in our hands, ready to give it up when we heard the call.

A pause.

HENRY. [*Opens door centre and enters. Sees* OCEANA *and halts.*] Oh!

OCEANA. [*Turns and sees him.*] Why! Here's a man! [*They gaze at each other, transfixed.*] Ethel! Who *is* he?

ETHEL. Why, this is Henry. Letitia's husband.

OCEANA. Oh! Letitia's husband! [*With a sudden, frank gesture, putting out her hand.*] Henry!

HENRY. Oceana!

As their hands meet, they stand looking into each other's faces.

OCEANA. [*Gripping his hand tightly.*] You are strong! [*Looks at his hand.*] And you do not smoke, either! Let me see your eyes.

HENRY. [*Perplexed.*] My eyes?

OCEANA. Your eyes. [*Turns him toward the light; studies his eyes.*] They dosed you with quinine! Malaria, I suppose?

HENRY. Why . . . yes. But how can you tell?

OCEANA. I can tell many things. Let me see your tongue.

HENRY. [*Bewildered.*] My tongue?

OCEANA. Your tongue.

HENRY. But what for?

OCEANA. I can tell more about a man by looking at his tongue for a minute than by listening to it for a week.

HENRY. But, Oceana—

OCEANA. I am in earnest.

HENRY. [*Laughs.*] Why . . . really . . .

ACT II]   **THE NATUREWOMAN**   37

OCEANA. Are you afraid?

HENRY. Good heavens, no!

OCEANA. Put it out. [*He puts his tongue out and she examines it.*] So! A man with a red tongue! And in a civilized city!

HENRY. Oughtn't it to be red?

OCEANA. And he doesn't know what it ought to be! How delicious! [*She steps back from him.*] And so you are Letitia's husband. Tell me, are you happy with her?

HENRY. [*Startled; stares at her intently.*] No, no . . . you ought not to ask me that.

OCEANA. Why not?

HENRY. [*In a low voice.*] Because you know.

OCEANA. Yes, that's true. [*A pause; she changes the subject.*] I have heard my father speak of you often.

HENRY. He remembered me, did he? I was only twenty when he went away.

OCEANA. He said that he taught you to play singlestick.

HENRY. Ah yes, to be sure!

OCEANA. He taught me also.

HENRY. You?

OCEANA. It was our favorite game.

HENRY. It's a rather rough game for a woman.

OCEANA. I love it. We'll have a bout.

HENRY. I'm afraid . . . I don't think I could.

OCEANA. Why not?

HENRY. [*Laughs.*] I should find it a psychical impossibility to hit a woman.

OCEANA. You might find it a physical impossibility in this case. [*With sudden excitement.*] Why, my trunks have come! We could have a go before dinner. Couldn't we, Freddy?

FREDDY. I suppose so.

OCEANA. Oh, it's just what I'm pining for! To get my blood stirring again! And you, too . . . surely you must be chafing, out of patience! [*She stops abruptly.*] Oh!

MRS. MASTERSON. [*Enters left.*] Henry!

HENRY. Yes?

MRS. MASTERSON. When did you get here?

HENRY. Just a minute ago.

MRS. MASTERSON. You've met Anna, I see.

OCEANA. Yes, Aunt Sophronia . . . we're getting along famously.

MRS. MASTERSON. Letitia's looking for you, Henry.

HENRY. Where is she?

MRS. MASTERSON. She went home to find you.

HENRY. Humph! I came here for her.

MRS. MASTERSON. She wants you at once.

HENRY. All right. Good-bye, Oceana.

OCEANA. Until later.

HENRY *exit centre with* MRS. MASTERSON.

OCEANA. So that is Henry! Tell me, Ethel, have they any children?

ETHEL. Yes . . . two.

OCEANA. How long have they been married?

ETHEL. Six years.

OCEANA. Six years! And is he really happy?

ETHEL. Why . . . you know Letitia.

OCEANA. Yes, but I don't know Henry.

ETHEL. [*Laughs.*] I guess he's so-so. Like most of us.

OCEANA. [*Half to herself.*] I'll find out for myself. *Phone rings;* FREDDY *rises.*] What's that? It's the 'phone. [*Rises.*] I hadn't noticed it before! How interesting!

ETHEL. That's so! You never saw one?

FREDDY. [*At 'phone.*] Hello! Yes, this is Mrs. Masterson's. This is her son. Can't I take the message? Oh, from Miss Pilkington. Oh! Why, that's too bad! Why no, of course not. Tell Miss Pilkington we're as sorry as can be! No, I'll attend to it. Good-bye. [*Turns.*] Miss Pilkington can't come!

ETHEL. What?

FREDDY. She's slipped in the snow and hurt her ankle.

ETHEL. Oh, Freddy!

OCEANA. What a shame!

They stare at one another.

ETHEL. Was that she at the 'phone?

FREDDY. No, her maid. She's laid up.

ETHEL. What in the world will we do?

FREDDY. It's too late to notify people.

ETHEL. How perfectly beastly!

FREDDY. I'll go tell mother.

OCEANA. No, wait!

FREDDY. What is it?

OCEANA. I've an idea.

FREDDY. What?

OCEANA. Why not let *me* take her place?

ETHEL. How do you mean?

OCEANA. Let me dance!

ETHEL. Oh!

OCEANA. Why not? I'd love to do it.

ETHEL. Oceana! You'd do the Sunrise Dance?

OCEANA. Yes; and then if they liked it, I could do some others.

ETHEL. Oh, Oceana! How perfectly lovely! But . . . but I wonder if it would be all right. I mean . . . it wouldn't shock them?

OCEANA. Why should it, my dear?

ETHEL. Is it what they'd call proper?

OCEANA. Why, of course, Ethel. How ridiculous! It isn't a sex-dance. It's religious.

FREDDY. And the costume?
OCEANA. Oh, the costume is **beautiful**.
ETHEL. Then I'll ask mother.
Starts to go.
OCEANA. Wait. Will Henry be there?
ETHEL. Of course.
OCEANA. Are you sure?
ETHEL. Of course.
OCEANA. [*Eagerly.*] Why ask your mother at all? Why not just go ahead and do it?
ETHEL. Oceana!
OCEANA. Why not? She'd only worry meantime. So let's just wait, and I'll go ahead.
ETHEL. Oh, would you dare?
OCEANA. Why, of course! She needn't know until almost time. Is this Miss Pilkington known here?
ETHEL. No, she's never been in Boston before.
FREDDY. Mother met her in London. She promised she'd do her famous Biblical Dances for mother's pet foundling asylum.
OCEANA. Well, don't you see? Most of the people wouldn't know till it was all over! And oh, Ethel, it would be such a lark! [ETHEL *and* FREDDY *gaze at each other dubiously.*] Who was going to play for Miss Pilkington?
ETHEL. I was.
OCEANA. Well, then, you can play for me! You see, Ethel, I'm afraid to tell your mother . . . she mightn't be willing. She wants to suppress me, and oh, I just can't be suppressed! I must have something to do or I'll jump out of my skin, Ethel. Truly, my dear, if this goes on much longer, I'll go out and climb the telegraph pole in front of the house! And if I can only make an impression with my dancing, then I may choose that for my career. I've been thinking of it seriously . . . it's one way

that people might let me preach joy and health to them. If I can't do that, I'll go off and turn into a suffragette, or join the Anarchists, or something worse!

ETHEL. Freddy, what do you say?

FREDDY. I'll stand my share of the racket.

OCEANA. Oh, come on! I'm just wild for some kind of mischief! I could dance like the grandmother of all the witches! Come, let's practice some. Play for me, Ethel! Play! [*Pushes her toward the piano; raises her hands in triumph; whispers.*] Henry!

CURTAIN

ACT III

Front part of stage shows an ante-room, with folding doors opening to rear part, which represents a portion of the Masterson parlor, curtained off to form a stage for the dance. Entrances down stage right and left. Up stage, at the left, are the curtains, which part in the middle; they are held by a cord which is fastened by the wall. OCEANA'S *trunk stands near entrance, right. Also a couple of chairs.*

At rise: FREDDY *stands left, holding curtain cord.* OCEANA *lies up centre, covered with the "Bridal-robe," asleep. Music of Sunrise Dance begins softly.* FREDDY *draws back curtains, revealing part of audience, left. He steals off.* OCEANA *gradually awakens, raises her head, lifts herself to her knees, stretches out her hands in worship to the Sun-god. Then slowly she rises, rapt in wonder. The robe falls back, revealing a filmy costume, primitive, elemental, naïve. She begins to sway, and gradually glides into an ecstatic dance, which portrays the joyful awakening of morning.*

MRS. MASTERSON. [*Enters, left, in great agitation, stares at* OCEANA, *wrings her hands, paces about, signals to her frantically.*] Oh! Oh!
    Rushes left and releases curtains, which fall.
OCEANA. [*Turns in consternation.*] Why! What . . . [*Sees* MRS. MASTERSON.] Aunt Sophronia!
MRS. MASTERSON. How dare you! How dare **you!**

OCEANA. Why, what's the matter?

MRS. MASTERSON. You ask me? Oh, oh!

OCEANA. Aunt Sophronia, you stopped my dance!

MRS. MASTERSON. Hussy! Shameless wanton! You have disgraced me before all the world!

OCEANA. [*Stares at her, slowly comprehending.*] Oh! I see! [*Goes to her with signs of distress.*] Oh, Aunt Sophronia, I'm so sorry! I didn't mean to displease you!

MRS. MASTERSON. Such a humiliation!

OCEANA. Aunt Sophronia, you must believe me . . . I had a reason!

MRS. MASTERSON. A *what?*

OCEANA. A reason for doing it! I couldn't help it . . . believe me, believe me!

MRS. MASTERSON. But what . . . what reason? What do you mean?

OCEANA. I can't tell you, Aunt Sophronia. But truly . . . if you knew, you would understand. I simply *had* to do it.

MRS. MASTERSON. [*Bewildered.*] Is the girl mad?

OCEANA. Yes, I believe that is it! I am mad!

DR. MASTERSON. [*Opens door and enters left.*] Oceana!

MRS. MASTERSON. [*Hurries to him.*] Quincy! Don't come in here! It's not decent! [*Pushes him towards door; to* OCEANA.] Put something on you, girl!

OCEANA. Of course. [*Puts on robe.*]

MRS. MASTERSON. I can't comprehend you! Have you no sense of shame whatever?

OCEANA. I had a sense of shame.

MRS. MASTERSON. Naked! Almost naked! And in my home!

ETHEL. [*Enters left.*] Mother, what's the matter?

MRS. MASTERSON. Ethel! You knew of this outrageous plot . . .

OCEANA. One moment, Aunt Sophronia. The blame for this rests upon me alone. I told Ethel that the dance was all right.

MRS. MASTERSON. Ethel, leave the room. This is no place for you.

ETHEL. Mother! The people are waiting . . .

MRS. MASTERSON. Go at once! [*To* DR. MASTERSON.] Quincy, go out and make some apology to our guests. Explain to them that we had no idea . . . we were imposed upon . . .

Applause heard off left.

OCEANA. Perhaps if your guests were consulted . . .

DR. MASTERSON. My dear Sophronia . . .

MRS. MASTERSON. [*Pushes him off.*] Go! Quickly! [*Turns to* OCEANA.] And as for you, Anna Talbot, there is no more to be said. You have overwhelmed me with shame.

OCEANA. Perhaps, Aunt Sophronia, you would prefer I should leave your house?

MRS. MASTERSON. [*Stiffly.*] I would make no objection.

OCEANA. I will go as soon as I dress.

MRS. MASTERSON. Very well. [*Starts towards the door.*] I will do what I can to atone for your wantonness.

OCEANA. One moment, Aunt Sophronia.

MRS. MASTERSON. Well?

OCEANA. Ethel tells me that you had something to say to me about grandfather's will.

MRS. MASTERSON. Oh! Ethel told you, did she?

OCEANA. Yes . . . she wished you to know that she had told me. Of course, feeling towards me as you do, you would hardly expect me to give up any rights that I may have.

MRS. MASTERSON. We will be content with what rights the law allows us.

ACT III] THE NATUREWOMAN

OCEANA. What I wished to say was that I would be willing to give Ethel part of my inheritance.

MRS. MASTERSON. Oh!

OCEANA. I would not give it to Freddy, for he is a man, and I should be breaking the mainspring of his life. But I will give half my money to Ethel, provided that you will consent to let her go with me.

MRS. MASTERSON. Oh! So that is your idea! You have already weaned the child from me . . . you have made her a traitor to me; and now you wish to buy her altogether.

OCEANA. Aunt Sophronia!

MRS. MASTERSON. Your offer is declined. I have no more to say to you.

She sweeps out.

OCEANA. [*Stands lost in thought; a smile grows upon her face.*] Poor Aunt Sophronia!

Begins to hum, and to sway as in the Sunrise Dance. She completes the dance from where she was interrupted, from an impulse of inner delight.

FREDDY. [*Steals in right; watches her, enraptured, as she stands with arms outstretched in ecstasy. He rushes towards her and flings himself at her feet, clasping her hand.*] Oceana!

OCEANA. Freddy!

FREDDY. [*Sobbing incoherently.*] Oceana! I can't stand it!

OCEANA. Why . . . what's the matter?

FREDDY. I love you! I love you! I can't live without you! I can't give you up . . . Oceana, have mercy on me!

OCEANA. [*Gravely.*] Freddy! This won't do! No . . . let go of me, please! You must control yourself.

FREDDY. Don't send me away! How can you be so cruel to me?

OCEANA. But, Freddy, I have told you that I don't love you. [*She stands, thinking.*] Give me my robe. Now, come sit down here, and listen to me. I am going away, Freddy, and you won't see me any more. And that is for the best . . . for you must get me out of your mind. I don't love you, Freddy.

FREDDY. And you **never would love me**?

OCEANA. Never.

FREDDY. But why not . . . why not?

OCEANA. I can't tell you that.

FREDDY. Oh, you are pitiless to me!

OCEANA. One does not give love out of pity. That is a cowardly thing to ask. [*She pauses.*] I must be frank with you, Freddy. You have got to face the facts. When I give my love, it will be to a man; and you are not a man.

FREDDY. But I am growing up!

OCEANA. No; you don't understand me. You should have grown up years ago. You have been stunted. [*She takes his hand.*] Look! See the stains!

FREDDY. Why . . .

OCEANA. Cigarettes! And you want to be a man!

FREDDY. Is that so unforgivable?

OCEANA. It is only one thing of many, my dear cousin.

FREDDY. Oceana, you don't know what men are!

OCEANA. Oh, don't I! My dear boy, there is nothing about men that I don't know. I have read Krafft-Ebing and Havelock Ellis . . . I know it all. I know it as a physician knows it. I can read a man's diseases in his complexion . . . I can read his vices in his eyes. Don't you see?

FREDDY. [*Drops his eyes.*] I see!

OCEANA. Don't think that I am despising you, dear boy. I know the world you have lived in.

FREDDY. But what can I *do?*

ACT III] THE NATUREWOMAN 47

OCEANA. You can go away, and make a man of yourself. Go West, get out into the open. Learn to ride and hunt . . harden your muscles and expand your chest. Until then you're not fit to be the father of any woman's child!

FREDDY. Drop college, you mean?

OCEANA. Be your own college! The idea of trying to build a brain in a body that's decaying! How could you stand it? Don't you ever feel that you are boiling over . . . that you must have something upon which you can wreak yourself? Don't you feel that you'd like to tame a horse, or to sail a boat in a storm? Don't you ever read about adventures?

FREDDY. Yes, I read about them.

OCEANA. And don't you ever feel that you must experience them? That you must face some kind of danger . . . do something that you can look back on with pride? Why, see . . . six years ago there came to our island three war-canoes full of savages . . . cannibals they were. If father and I hadn't been there, they'd have wiped our people out. And do you think I'd give up the memory of that struggle?

FREDDY. What happened?

OCEANA. Fortunately they came in the daytime, so we soon drove them back to their boats. See . . . I'll show you. [*She goes to trunk.*] Here's one of them.

She lifts up a human skull.

FREDDY. Good Lord!

OCEANA. Notice that crack. That was done with a spear . . by my prince, the one who made me this robe, you know. He cleaned the skull out for me.

FREDDY. Rather a ghastly sort of souvenir.

OCEANA. Oh, I don't mind that. Father and I found it useful . . . a sort of *memento mori*.

FREDDY. [*Looking into trunk.*] And what are those things?

OCEANA. They are some of my arrows. And these are what we used for bowls . . . turtle-shells, you see.

FREDDY. [*Pointing.*] But those?

OCEANA. Oh, my single-sticks. [*Lifts them.*] That's the game Henry and I were talking about. You ought to get him to teach it to you.

FREDDY. What's it like?

OCEANA. I'll show you. [*She takes from the trunk two leather helmets and gloves.*] Here you are! It's an old English game . . . didn't you ever read "Robin Hood"?

FREDDY. Oh, it's that? Why, they used to crack each other's heads!

OCEANA. The object was to draw first blood. But we used to wear these helmets. You see how we've dented them up? And these old cudgels . . . how they remind me of father!

FREDDY. Humph! They're heavy.

OCEANA. You take the stick this way; it's a kind of fencing. [*She gives him a stick and illustrates the play.*] No, so!

MRS. MASTERSON. [*Enters.*] What's this? Is this the way you get ready to leave?

OCEANA. [*Imploring.*] Oh, Aunt Sophronia, I beg your pardon! I got so interested . . .

MRS. MASTERSON. Is there no limit to your indiscretion?

DR. MASTERSON. [*Enters hurriedly.*] Sophronia, I beg of you . . .

MRS. MASTERSON. I will hear no more of this! I have spoken, once for all . . .

DR. MASTERSON. But, my dear . . .

MRS. MASTERSON. No more!

DR. MASTERSON. But, Sophronia, the people don't understand why . . .

MRS. MASTERSON. It was outrageous!

DR. MASTERSON. I know. But since it was begun . . . it's so difficult to explain . . .

MRS. MASTERSON. No more of this! I won't hear it!

HENRY. [*Enters; stares about.*] Mrs. Masterson, what have you done here?

MRS. MASTERSON. There is no reason why you should concern yourself with it.

HENRY. But I wish to know.

MRS. MASTERSON. What do you wish to know?

HENRY. Did you stop Oceana's dance?

MRS. MASTERSON. I did.

HENRY. And why?

MRS. MASTERSON. Because I saw fit to.

HENRY. But your guests . . .

MRS. MASTERSON. I will attend to my guests.

HENRY. But what is Oceana going to do?

MRS. MASTERSON. She is going to leave our house.

HENRY. This is a shame. Most of the people enjoyed the dance. They would like to see more . . .

MRS. MASTERSON. Henry, you will permit me to decide about what goes on in my home.

HENRY. You may decide for yourself. But if Oceana leaves to-night, I will leave also . . . and I will never return.

MRS. MASTERSON. Very well, sir; as you please.

OCEANA. Henry, let me have a say. I am obliged to you, but I don't want to stay. It's absurd for me to be here . . . I don't belong here. I've lived all my life under the open sky; I've been free. I've swum several miles every day and run several more; I've hunted and fished and danced and played; and here they dress me up in long skirts and sit me in a corner and tell me I'm a lady! I can stand it just so long . . . I've stood it twenty-four hours, and I feel like a wild animal in a cage. If I don't find something to do . . . something real . . . something that is thrilling . . . truly, I'll murder some one. [*She paces the room;* DR. *and* MRS. MASTERSON *shrink away from her.*] Yes, I mean it! [*With increasing vehemence.*] Picture me at home. When I was hungry, I went out for game; and unless I got the game, I stayed hungry. Or I went fishing, and I had to get my canoe through the surf. I had the zest of danger . . I had real struggle. But here I have nothing. They bring me my food on silver platters; they get up and give me their seats, they even push the doors open in front of me! And so I'm panting for something to do . . . for some opposition, some competition, some conflict. I'm spoiling for a fight! You, Henry, don't you know what I mean? A fight! [*With a sharp swift gesture.*] I want to meet some wild animal again! Is there a wild animal in you? [*They stare at each other; suddenly she springs and takes the other single stick from* FREDDY.] Here! You know this game! My father taught you! [*She holds out one to him.*] Come on!

HENRY. [*Bewildered.*] Oceana! This is not the place.

OCEANA. It's the place for me! Take it! [*She forces it on him.*] Now! Forget that I'm a woman! Ready!

HENRY. Oceana! No!

OCEANA. Are you afraid of your mother-in-law?

HENRY. Good heavens!

OCEANA. If you're not, you're the only man in the family that isn't. [*She drops her robe.*] Now!

MRS. MASTERSON. This is disgraceful!

DR. MASTERSON. Oceana, I beg of you . . .

OCEANA. Defend yourself! [*She makes a feint at* HENRY's *head, causing him to raise his stick.*] Lay on!

She attacks him briskly. He defends himself. There is a swift rattle of the sticks and a vivid conflict.

ACT III] **THE NATUREWOMAN** 51

HENRY. [*Laughing.*] Oceana, for God's sake, stop!
MRS. MASTERSON. Oh, stop them!
DR. MASTERSON. Are you mad?
FREDDY. Oceana!
OCEANA. [*Wild with the excitement of the struggle.*] Lay on! Ha, ha! Well played! Guard! Once again! Ah, this is what I like! This is what I've been looking for!
  They leap here and there; the others dodge out of the way, protesting; the conflict grows more and more strenuous.
LETITIA. [*Enters left; screams in terror.*] Henry! [*They stop; a long pause.*] Henry! What does this mean?
HENRY. My dear . . .
  Stops for lack of breath.
OCEANA. Freddy, my robe.
  Wraps herself and sits in chair, smiling.
LETITIA. What does this mean?
MRS. MASTERSON. Of all the shameless and insane procedures!
LETITIA. Are you mad, Henry?
OCEANA. No, no, Letitia. We know just what we're about. You see, your husband and I are considering whether or not we shall fall in love with each other.
LETITIA. [*Wildly.*] Oh!
MRS. MASTERSON. Monstrous!
DR. MASTERSON. Oceana!
LETITIA. How dare you?
OCEANA. He's interested, you know. I've got hold of him.
LETITIA. [*Furiously.*] Henry, you stand there and permit her to insult me . . .
HENRY. My dear, believe me . . .
OCEANA. [*Sharply.*] Stop, Henry! [*A pause.*] Look at me!

HENRY. Well?

OCEANA. Don't tell her a lie. A lie is the thing I never pardon.

HENRY. Why . . . why . . .

Falls silent.

MRS. MASTERSON. Henry!

FREDDY. Gee whiz!

LETITIA. Henry, I demand that you come home with me instantly.

OCEANA. Don't go.

LETITIA. [*Almost speechless.*] If you stay here, you stay alone!

OCEANA. [*Rises, casts aside her robe, stretches wide her arms.*] Letitia! Look at me! Am I the sort of woman that you can safely leave your husband alone with?

LETITIA. [*Stares at her terrified, then bursts into tears and flings herself into* HENRY's *arms.*] Henry!

OCEANA. Ah, yes! That is safer!

HENRY. [*Supports* LETITIA.] My dear! My dear!

LETITIA. Come home with me!

OCEANA. God, man, how I pity you! Bound in chains to a woman like that! And with all the world conspiring to hold you fast! How can you bear it? Do you expect to bear it forever? What will become of your soul? Oh, I pity you! I pity you!

LETITIA. [*Hysterically.*] Henry, take me home! Take me home at once!

HENRY. Yes, my dear, yes!

OCEANA. What is the spell they've laid upon you? You make me think of Gulliver . . . a giant stretched out upon the ground, impotent, bound fast with a million tiny threads! Wake up, man . . . wake up! You've only one life to live. You act as if you had a thousand.

LETITIA. Mother!

MRS. MASTERSON. How long is this to continue?

LETITIA. Henry, *won't* you stop listening to her?

OCEANA. He's not listening to me, Letitia. He's listening to the voice of the universe, calling to him. The voice of unborn generations, clamoring, agonizing! What do you suppose it means, man . . . this storm that has shaken us? It is Nature's trumpet-call . . . it is the shout of discovery of the powers within us! For ages upon ages life has been preparing it . . . and now suddenly we meet . . . the barriers are shattered and flung down, the tides of being sweep us together!

MRS. MASTERSON. Oh! This is outrageous!

DR. MASTERSON. Oceana, Henry is married!

OCEANA. Married! Married! That is the sorcery with which you bind him! No longer a man at all, but some aborted thing . . . a relic! an eunuch! They mumble their incantations over you . . . the spell is done, and you sink back, cowed and whimpering! You are a machine, a domestic utensil! Never again are you to love and to dare and to create! No, there are other things in life for you . . . bread and butter, cooks and dinner parties, billiards and bridge-whist . . . that is your portion! A married man!

LETITIA. [*Terrified.*] Henry! For God's sake!

He no longer returns her embraces, but stares at OCEANA, *fascinated.*

OCEANA. Don't you see, man? It's a dream! A nightmare! Rouse yourself, lift your head . . . and it's gone! Life is calling! Come away!

LETITIA. [*Frantically.*] Mother! Mother!

MRS. MASTERSON. Quincy, if you can't stop this outrage, I will! Call the servants!

She starts toward OCEANA.

OCEANA. Call the police! Call your guests! Anything

. . . bring the world down on him. Terrify him with conventions, beat him into subjection again!

MRS. MASTERSON. Wanton!

OCEANA. Wanton! Oh, how well you understand me! I, with my hunger for righteousness . . . I, who have disciplined myself as an anchorite, who have served as a priestess of life! And you, with your formulas and your superstitions . . . you pass judgment upon me! [*With terrific energy.*] See! This man and I, we are the gateway to the future! And you seek to bar it! By what right do you stand in the path of posterity . . . you tormentors of the ideal, you assassins of human hope!

MRS. MASTERSON. [*Almost striking her.*] Oh! *Oh!* And my children have to listen to this! [*She whirls about.*] Ethel! Freddy! Go out of the room!

ETHEL. *I* am going with Oceana.

MRS. MASTERSON. *What?*

ETHEL. Some day . . . if not now. She's perfectly right. Letitia has no business to keep him. She never would have got him if she hadn't played a part.

MRS. MASTERSON. Ethel Masterson!

LETITIA. Little vixen!

FREDDY. [*Rushes to* OCEANA *and seizes her hand.*] Oceana! Let me go with you, too!

DR. MASTERSON. What *next?*

OCEANA. No, Freddy . . . no! [*She withdraws her hand and holds it out to* HENRY.] Henry! Come!

A tense pause; all stare at HENRY. *He never takes his eyes from* OCEANA. *Slowly, like one hypnotized, he draws away from his wife's embrace, and moves towards* OCEANA. *He seizes her hand. All stand transfixed. Silence.*

CURTAIN

ACT IV

The scene shows the living-room of a bungalow. Large stone fireplace centre; windows and window seats on each side; French windows leading to piazza right; piano between them; door left to another room; large mirror beside it. Centre table, rustic chairs, deer-heads and skins, Indian blankets, etc.
At rise: The stage is empty.

OCEANA. [*Laughs off.*] Oh, say, but that was an adventure!
    Enters; glowing and exultant from a long mountain walk. She wears a "Rosalind" costume, brown, with soft boots, gauntlet gloves and light fur about the neck; carries a pair of snow-shoes, which she has taken off, and from which she knocks the snow.
HENRY. [*Follows.*] You like the mountains!
OCEANA. Oh, my dear! They are marvellous! I've never imagined anything like it . . . to be able to see so much of the world at once. It's the way you think of heaven.
HENRY. You don't mind the cold?
OCEANA. I find I prefer it. I think I shall stay here forever. It tunes you up so! It makes you quite drunk! [*Looks at herself in the mirror.*] I look cute in this, don't I?
HENRY. You look like a fairy-story!
OCEANA. I ought to have had sense enough to think of a theatrical costumer in the beginning. [*Stretches her arms.*] Oh, I feel so wonderful! Ha, ha, ha! I don't

know whether it's the mountain air . . . or whether it's because I'm in love!

HENRY. [*Seizes her hand.*] Sweetheart!

OCEANA. [*Stares at him.*] How wonderful it is! Beyond all believing! I'm stunned by it . . . afraid of it. Tell me, Hal, were you ever drunk?

HENRY. [*Laughs.*] Once or twice.

OCEANA. [*Seriously.*] I never was. But I've watched my people sometimes and tried to understand it. And it's just that. Nature has made us drunk!

HENRY. And that is what frightens you?

OCEANA. She has her purposes, Hal; and I don't want to be her blind victim. But then, I look at you again, and wonder leaps up in me . . . love, such as I never conceived of before; power . . . vision without end. I seem to be a hundred times myself! It is as if barriers were broken down within me . . . I see into new vistas of life. I understand . . . I exult! Oh, Hal, I shall never be the same again!

HENRY. Nor I; I look back at myself as I was a week ago, and I can't believe it!

OCEANA. With me it is like a great fountain inside. It surges up, and I cannot be still! I want to laugh . . . to sing! I have to dance it out of me! Do you know Anitra's Dance, Hal?

HENRY. Yes, of course.

OCEANA. [*Begins to sing the music to herself and playfully to dance. The enthusiasm of it takes hold of her, and she dances more quickly.*] Play it, Hal! Play! [HENRY *sits at piano and plays Anitra's Dance; she dances tumultuously, ending in a whirlwind of excitement.*] Oh!

    As HENRY *rises, she flies to him and he clasps her passionately.*

HENRY. Sweetheart!

OCEANA. [*Panting.*] Oh, Hal, I'm so happy! so happy!

[*She sobs upon his shoulder, then looks at him through her tears.*] Oh, if I only dared let myself go!

HENRY. Why not, dearest?

OCEANA. It sweeps me off my feet! And I have to hold myself in.

HENRY. Why? Don't I love you?

OCEANA. Yes, I know. But I'm terrified at myself; I'm losing my self-control. And I promised father.

HENRY. What?

OCEANA. That I would never do it. "Never feel an emotion," he would say, "that you could not stop feeling if you wished to."

HENRY. But, sweetheart . . . why so much distrust? Why should we wait, when everything in us cries out against it?

OCEANA. Don't say that to me now, Hal!

HENRY. But why not?

OCEANA. This is not the time for such a thought. You know it!

HENRY. Dearest . . .

OCEANA. [*Passionately.*] Ah, don't put it all on me! Don't make it too hard for me!

HENRY. But if I only knew . . .

OCEANA. You will know before long. Ah, Hal, see how I'm situated. I've broken all the laws. I've no precedent to help me . . . I have to work it all out for myself. I shall have to bear the scorn of the world; and oh, think if I had to bear the scorn of my own conscience! Don't you see?

HENRY. Yes, I see. But . . .

OCEANA. I have chosen a certain course. I have forced myself to be calm, to think it out in the cold light of reason, to decide what is *right* for me to do. And now I must keep to my resolution. You would not want our love to lead me into shame!

HENRY. No!

OCEANA. Do you read Nietzsche, Henry?

HENRY. He is a mere name to me.

OCEANA. I will give you some lines of Nietzsche's. "Canst thou give thyself thy good and thine evil, and hang thy will above thee as thy law? Canst thou be thine own judge, and avenger of thy law? Fearful is it to be alone with the judge and the avenger of thy law. So is a stone flung out into empty space and into the icy breath of isolation."

HENRY. That's all right . . . but if you expect Letitia to face this problem in any such way, you will be sadly disappointed.

OCEANA. That's none of my affair. All I have to do is to give her a chance. If she cannot face the facts, she has passed sentence upon herself.

HENRY. [*Laughs.*] All right, my dear. It will certainly be a scene to watch!

OCEANA. You think she will come?

HENRY. Oh, she'll certainly come.

OCEANA. And she won't bring her mother?

HENRY. I can't tell about that.

OCEANA. If she does, we'll simply have to send her down to the village . . . I won't talk in Aunt Sophronia's presence.

HENRY. I was perfectly explicit on that point. [*Takes paper from table.*] Here's the telegram: "Come to the bungalow immediately, upon a matter of extreme urgency. Do not bring your mother."

OCEANA. Certainly that is clear enough.

HENRY. And bewildering enough. But I suppose they are prepared for anything by now.

OCEANA. It's past the time. [*Looking from window.*] We should be able to see a sleigh.

HENRY. No, the road turns behind that hillock there.

OCEANA. But look!
HENRY. What?
OCEANA. There's some one coming afoot.
HENRY. Where?
OCEANA. Round that side! By the path! Why, it's Ethel!
HENRY. Good Lord! Ethel!
OCEANA. She's come up from the village afoot.
HENRY. Well, of all the apparitions!
OCEANA. Run help her, Henry. She's running. [*Opens window and calls.*] Ethel! [HENRY *exit hurriedly.*] Why, the poor, dear child! I wonder if she came in Letitia's stead! But then . . . why wouldn't she get a sleigh? [*Calls.*] Ethel! What's the matter?
HENRY. [*Off.*] She says Letitia is coming!
OCEANA. Oh!
HENRY. She's just behind!
OCEANA. But, Ethel, what are you doing here?
ETHEL. [*Off, breathless.*] Wait!
OCEANA. Why, you poor child, you're exhausted. What in the world . . .
ETHEL. Wait.
 Enters, breathless, half carried by HENRY.
OCEANA. [*Pounces upon her.*] Ethel! Of all the surprises! You dear thing! [*Embraces her, shakes snow from her.*] What in the world has happened?
ETHEL. Oceana, I ran away!
OCEANA. You ran away?
ETHEL. To you! I couldn't stand it! I must be with you, Oceana—no matter how wicked it is, I must be with you!
OCEANA. [*Breathlessly.*] Ethel!
ETHEL. Yes, I'm desperate . . . I'll die if I have to stay at home.
OCEANA. My dear, dear girl! [*Clasps her.*]

ETHEL. You won't send me back?
OCEANA. Never!
ETHEL. [*Wildly.*] But, Oceana, Letitia is coming!
OCEANA. Yes?
ETHEL. I took a train from Boston. And when I saw her come aboard, imagine how I felt! I hid . . . she d n't see me. And I got off the train first and dodged out of sight. I ran all the way. I suppose she stopped to get a sleigh.
HENRY. It's all right, Ethel . . . we knew she was coming.
ETHEL. You *knew* it?
OCEANA. Yes, Henry sent for her. You see, Letitia and I have to talk things out.
ETHEL. Well, of all the . . .

Stops, dazed.

OCEANA. [*Laughs.*] That's all right, dear. We know what we're doing. But it was good of you to try to save us!
HENRY. Listen!
OCEANA. Ah!
HENRY. The sleigh-bells!
OCEANA. She's here!
ETHEL. [*Clasping her.*] Oceana!
OCEANA. What is it, dear?
ETHEL. Don't let her take me back home?
OCEANA. But how can she take you, dear, if you won't go?
ETHEL. She might persuade you.
OCEANA. Never fear, Ethel . . . we'll stand by you, won't we, Hal?
HENRY. Yes.
ETHEL. She'll threaten to *make* me go.
OCEANA. Her mind will be taken up with other things, Ethel.

ETHEL. But mother will come! And she'll command me to return. I'm not of age, you know.

OCEANA. But then, if you won't obey? Will she send for the police?

ETHEL. No . . . hardly that.

OCEANA. All right, then, dear. I'll save you . . . trust me. I mean to give you a chance for life.

ETHEL. And, oh, Oceana . . . what do you think? Freddy's run away, too!

OCEANA. *What?*

HENRY. Where to?

ETHEL. He's gone out West!

OCEANA. You don't mean it!

HENRY. What for?

ETHEL. He says he's going to be a cowboy. He's going to make a man of himself. He left a letter to father.

OCEANA. Why, the dear boy!

ETHEL. [*Mysteriously.*] Oceana, do you know what was the matter?

OCEANA. No . . . what?

ETHEL. I think I know. He was in love with you!

OCEANA. I shouldn't wonder, my dear. [*Laughs.*] But don't tell Henry . . . he'll be jealous!

Sound of sleigh-bells louder.

ETHEL. Here she is!

OCEANA. You go into the next room now. It wouldn't be considered proper for you to hear what we're going to say.

ETHEL. Of all the adventures!

Exit.

OCEANA. [*Smiles at Henry.*] Now then!

HENRY. You wanted it, my dear!

They turn, gazing right. The sleigh-bells have come nearer, then stopped. Some one is heard to step upon the piazza and stamp the snow from the feet.

LETITIA. [*Enters right, stares at* OCEANA *and screams.*] Oceana!

OCEANA. Letitia . . .

LETITIA. [*Gasps for breath.*] Henry! How dared you bring me here to meet that woman?

OCEANA. Letitia . . .

LETITIA. Don't speak to me! Don't you dare to speak to me! [*She sinks down by table and bursts into tears.*] Oh, how horrible! How horrible! As if I had not humiliations enough already!

HENRY. [*Taking step toward her.*] Letitia . . .

OCEANA. [*With a swift gesture.*] Wait!

LETITIA. Oh, who would have thought it possible! To bring me 'way up here . . .

OCEANA. You might as well understand at the outset . . . the thing cannot be done that way.

LETITIA. [*With concentrated hatred.*] You *dare!*

OCEANA. We have sent for you . . .

LETITIA. *We* have sent for you!

OCEANA. Because we wished to talk things out with you in a sensible way. And you'll have to make up your mind to control yourself.

LETITIA. [*Sobbing.*] Henry, you permit this shameful humiliation!

OCEANA. Henry has nothing to do with this affair, Letitia. It is I who have to talk to you.

LETITIA. [*Bursts into hysterical weeping again.*] Oh, that I should have lived to see this!

OCEANA. You will find out before you get through that I mean to deal with you fairly. But you cannot accomplish anything by hysterics.

LETITIA. Oh, oh, oh!

ACT IV] THE NATUREWOMAN 63

OCEANA. And you had best believe me; you injure your case by refusing to act rationally.

LETITIA. [*Looks up, frightened.*] What do you want with me?

OCEANA. [*Quietly.*] In the first place, Letitia, I want to convey to you the information that your husband's relationship and mine has so far been what you would call innocent.

LETITIA. *What?*

OCEANA. I was a virgin when I came to Boston, and I am a virgin still.

LETITIA. And you expect me to believe that?

OCEANA. My dear, I don't care in the least whether you believe it or not.

LETITIA. [*Faintly.*] But . . .

OCEANA. What reason would I have to fear you? He is mine, if I want him.

LETITIA. [*Dazed.*] Then what . . why are you here? Why . . .

OCEANA. I came here because I wished to get acquainted with him. And what chance have a man and woman to get acquainted with each other in the conventional world?

LETITIA. [*Stares at her; then, faintly.*] But what

OCEANA. I wished to try him out . . . in body, mind and soul. I wished to know if he was the man for me.

LETITIA. [*Rushes to* HENRY.] Oh! Have you no decency left? Have you no mercy on me? What has come over you?

HENRY. Letitia . . .

OCEANA. Let me attend to this, Hal.

LETITIA. *Hal!*

OCEANA. That a woman could be married to a man for six years and continue to call him Henry, speaks volumes for the romance of their relationship!

LETITIA. [*To* HENRY.] Where's your sense of shame?

OCEANA. You are taking the wrong line, Letitia. No such consideration has a moment's weight with us.

LETITIA. [*Catches her breath.*] Since it seems that I am here at your mercy, I ask to know your pleasure?

OCEANA. The reason that we have sent for you is that I might assure myself upon two points . . . first, as to whether your husband still loves you, and second, as to whether you still love him.

LETITIA. You doubt that I love him?

OCEANA. So far, Letitia, your actions have proceeded, not from love of him, but from hatred of me.

LETITIA. Oh! And if I fail to measure up to your tests of love . . .

OCEANA. [*Triumphantly.*] Then he is mine!

LETITIA. And the fact that he is my husband . . .

OCEANA. Is nothing!

LETITIA. The fact that he vowed to keep faith with me . . .

OCEANA. Is nothing!

LETITIA. That I am dependent upon him for support . . .

OCEANA. You have money of your own, Letitia.

LETITIA. Do you suppose I am thinking about *money?* I mean his protection.

OCEANA. A person who confesses to the need of protection has written himself down an inferior. [*A pause.*] You see, Letitia, times have changed; our ideas of marriage have changed. In the beginning a woman was a man's economic dependent; now that the man has become ashamed of that, he is made the woman's spiritual dependent. You play upon his sense of chivalry, his sympathy, his pity; and you prey upon him, you devour him alive. But the time has come when that must cease, Letitia . . . man will not always be a domestic appendage!

And you will simply have to face this new situation. Do you still possess your husband's love? Do you really love *him?* Nothing else will count . . . none of your "rights" . . . we are not afraid of man or devil.

LETITIA. [*Gasps.*] Oh! [*Turns to* HENRY.] Henry, will you tell me what all this means? Can it be that you assent to these outrageous ideas?

HENRY. I assent to them, Letitia. It may be that you still love me, but you have given me few signs of it. You have been . . . you are . . . a selfish woman.

LETITIA. Henry!

HENRY. How often do you give a thought to me . . . to the needs of my nature? You think of your whims and your prejudices; you think of your social position . . . of your "world" and its conventions. You think of what your mother approves, of what your father approves, of what this person will say and what that person will say. And I follow you about . . . I play my part in the hollow show that you call life; but all the time my heart is crying out in me . . . I am starving . . . starving!

LETITIA. [*Startled.*] Henry!

OCEANA. Ah! She is beginning to see it!

LETITIA. [*Stretches out her arms and totters towards him, weeping.*] Henry! I love you! [*Wildly.*] Believe me! Believe me! I love you! Don't you remember when you were ill three years ago . . . how I nursed you and watched over you? You knew that I loved you then. Why, you said I'd worn myself to a shadow! You kissed me, and told me I'd saved your life! And when I was ill myself, and you thought I was dying . . . didn't you realize that you loved *me?* And the children? Have you never given a thought to them? Are *they* nothing to you? And you to them? You know that you love them, Henry . . . you dare not deny it. Are they to be without a father all their lives? [*Falls into his arms.*] My husband! .

HENRY. [*Catches her, deeply moved.*] Letitia!

OCEANA. [*Has been watching them intently; now, startled and pained.*] Ah! I thought so! [*She turns away; supports herself by the table; whispers.*] That settles it!

LETITIA. Henry, if I have been selfish, I am sorry! I humble myself before you . . . I beg you for forgiveness! Henry, I *do* love you! Don't you believe me?

HENRY. [*Faintly.*] I believe you.

OCEANA. [*Clenches her hands and turns resolutely.*] You see, Hal, I knew it! [*He bows his head.*] You can't get away from her. [*She pauses.*] You understand it all now . . . what my instinct told me. You still love her, you still belong to her. You would have gone away with me, and you would still have been thinking about her—worrying about her. It would have been tearing your soul in half. [*She waits; he does not look at her; she goes on, half to convince herself.*] She is not big enough to give you up. She could not say, "Oceana is young and needs you; you love Oceana, and she will make you happy. Go with her." No, she would think of the world and its conventions . . . she would be jealous and bitter. She would eat her heart out . . . she would tear herself to pieces! And that would tear you to pieces . . . you could never forget it. And there are the children, Hal. It's true that you love them; you think about them all the time . . . I know, for you speak of them. And she could take them away from you, legally . . . how much chance would they ever have in life, if she and her mother had the bringing up of them? Don't you see, Hal? What can we do?

LETITIA. [*Clinging to* HENRY's *bosom.*] Henry, I love you!

OCEANA. I want to play the game generously, Letitia; but it is all I can do not to despise you . . . because he loves you, and it has meant so little to you, you have done so little in return. That is the curse of this thing you call marriage. You say to yourself that you've got him . . . the law and the conventions will keep him for you . . . and so you can treat him as you please. You'll take him off with you now, and you'll set to work to get right back where you were before . . . yes, she will, Hal. She'll try to wheedle you into backing down from this position. She will weep and she will scold. But you stand firm . . . stand firm! What we did was *right* . . . it was noble and true, and if more married people did such things, it would be better for them.

LETITIA. [*Clinging to* HENRY.] Henry, come home with me!

HENRY. All right, I'll come.

He does not lift his head.

OCEANA. Look at me. It's all right, Hal . . . it's all right.

She speaks with intensity; they gaze into each other's eyes.

HENRY. [*Stretches out his hand to her.*] Oceana . . . I'm sorry . . .

OCEANA. [*With sudden emotion.*] No, Hal! Go . . . go quickly! Please!

He goes out, right, with LETITIA; OCEANA *stands gazing straight ahead. Sound of sleigh-bells heard. Suddenly she sinks into a chair, bows her head upon the table, and bursts into tears.*

ETHEL. [*Opens door, left, and stands gazing at* OCEANA *in alarm, then runs to her and sinks upon her knees before her.*] Oceana!

OCEANA. [*Sobbing.*] He's gone! Gone!

ETHEL. He left you?

OCEANA. I gave him up! I sent him away. Oh, Ethel, Ethel . . . what am I going to do?

ETHEL. Oceana!

OCEANA. Oh, how I loved him! I didn't realize how I loved him! The whole face of the world was changed . . . and now, now . . . how shall I bear it? [*She stares ahead of her.*] Oh, Ethel, tell me I did right to give him up.

ETHEL. Why did you do it?

OCEANA. I saw he loved her, and I had to give him up. It would have been to tear his soul in half! But now that he's gone, I don't see how I can bear it! [*A pause; she is lost in thought; she whispers with great intensity.*] There is a vision . . . it haunts me . . . it cries out in me in a voice of agony!

ETHEL. What?

OCEANA. A little child! You have no idea . . . how real it was to me! It fell out of the skies upon me! The thought never left me. I heard its voice . . . its laughter; I saw its smile. It called to me all day, and it played with me in my dreams; I felt its little hands upon me . . . its lips upon my breast. And it's gone!

ETHEL. Your child!

OCEANA. And his! And think . . . think of the awfulness of it . . . it was hovering at the gates of life! It wanted to be! And I trembled . . . I suffered; at any moment I might have said the word, and it would have come. But I did not say the word . . . and it is gone. And now it will never come! Never . . . never! I have murdered the child! My child!

ETHEL. No, no, Oceana!

OCEANA. God! I can't understand it! What does it mean? Did it exist when I thought of it? Does it exist now? Who can tell me?

ETHEL. I don't know, Oceana.

OCEANA. The strangeness of it! Sometimes my whole being rises up in revolt . . . I could tear the skies apart, to wrest the secret from them! You see, we don't know

ACT IV]   THE NATUREWOMAN   69

anything. We don't know what's right, we don't know what's wrong. We're in a trap! [*She rises suddenly.*] No, no, I mustn't talk that way. I've lost my self-control. I let myself go, and I had no right to. Now, what shall I do? Wait, dear . . . let me think, let me think calmly. [*Stares about her.*] I want to remember what father said to me; what I promised to do. See, Ethel . . . the sun is setting. Look at the sky! And it's the last day of the month, isn't it?

ETHEL. Yes.

OCEANA. If father had been here we should have sat us down to one of our services! Look here. [*She goes to trunk, and takes out a human skull.*] Ah, old friend!

ETHEL. [*Shocked.*] Oceana!

OCEANA. He came from the Marquesas, I think. And here's where he was hit with the spear. You see? Sit down. [*She places the skull before her.*] See, Ethel— he used to smile. And now and then he had the toothache . . . see that? He took himself very seriously; he was all wrapped up in the things that went on in this little cracked skull. But he lacked imagination. He never foresaw that somebody would carry him off to the New Hampshire mountains, and make him the text for a Hamlet soliloquy. Alas, poor Yorick! He did not know that he was immortal, you see; that life proceeded from him . . . unrolling itself for generation after generation without end; that all that he did would be perpetuated . . . that where he sinned we would suffer, and where he fought we would be strong. He did not know that he was the creator, the mystic fountain of an unexplored stream . . . the maker of an endless future . . . [*She stops; a spasm of pain crosses her face.*] Oh, Ethel! [*Clasps her hand.*] It is terrible to die young, is it not?

ETHEL. Yes.

OCEANA. Then how much worse is it to die before you

are born! To be strangled in the idea . . . to be stifled by a cowardly thought!

ETHEL. What do you mean?

OCEANA. Oh, Ethel, stay by me, will you? Promise me you will stay by me.

ETHEL. I will!

OCEANA. I'm frightened, Ethel . . . frightened at myself. I've done wrong . . . I've committed a crime! I ought not to have let him go! I ought not to have let him go!

ETHEL. Henry?

OCEANA. No, we mustn't speak of him again. I can't bear to hear his name. I have failed . . . I have failed. I've been crushed by civilization! [*Starts up.*] But there's my island! There's the white beach, shining in the moonlight, and the great breakers rolling in, and the palm trees rustling in the wind. Let us go together . . . to my island! Let us go back and get healed, before we try to face this world again!

CURTAIN

THE MACHINE

CHARACTERS

(In order of appearance)

JULIA PATTERSON: a magazine writer.
JACK BULLEN: a parlor Socialist.
LAURA HEGAN: Hegan's daughter.
ALLAN MONTAGUE: a lawyer.
JIM HEGAN: the traction king.
ANNIE ROBERTS: a girl of the slums.
ROBERT GRIMES: the boss.
ANDREWS: Hegan's secretary.
PARKER: a clerk.

ACT I

Julia Patterson's apartments in a model tenement on the lower East Side.

ACT II

Library at "The Towers," Hegan's country place on Long Island, two weeks later.

ACT III

Hegan's private office in Wall street, the next morning.

THE MACHINE

ACT I

JULIA PATTERSON'S *apartments in a model tenement on the lower East Side. The scene shows the living-room, furnished very plainly, but in the newest taste; "arts and crafts" furniture, portraits of Morris and Ruskin on the walls; a centre table, a couple of easy-chairs, a divan and many book-shelves. The entrance from the outer hall is at centre; entrance to the other rooms right and left.*

At rise: JULIA *has pushed back the lamp from the table and is having a light supper, with a cup of tea; and at the same time trying to read a magazine, which obstinately refuses to remain open at the right place. She is an attractive and intelligent woman of thirty. The doorbell rings.*

JULIA. Ah, Jack!
Presses button, then goes to the door.
JACK. [*Enters, having come upstairs at a run. He is a college graduate and volunteer revolutionist, one of the organizers of the "Society of the Friends of Russian Freedom"; handsome and ardent, eager in manner, and a great talker.*] Hello, Julia. All alone?
JULIA. Yes. I expected a friend, but she can't come until later.
JACK. Just eating?
JULIA. I've been on the go all day. Have something.

JACK. No; I had dinner. [*As she starts to clear things away.*] Don't stop on my account.

JULIA. I was just finishing up. [*As he begins to help.*] No; sit down.

JACK. Nonsense. Let the men be of some use in the world.

JULIA. What have you been up to to-day?

JACK. We're organizing a demonstration for the Swedish strikers.

JULIA. It's marvelous how those Swedes hold on, isn't it?

JACK. The people are getting their eyes open. And when they're once open, they stay open.

JULIA. Yes. Did you see my article?

JACK. I should think I did! Julia, that was a dandy!

JULIA. Do you think so?

JACK. I do, indeed. You've made a hit. I heard a dozen people talking about it.

JULIA. Indeed?

JACK. You've come to be the champion female muckraker of the country, I think.

JULIA *laughs.*

JACK. Why did you want to see me so specially to-night?

JULIA. I've a friend I want you to meet. Somebody I'm engaged in educating.

JACK. You seem to have chosen me for your favorite proselytizer.

JULIA. You've seen things with your own eyes, Jack.

JACK. Yes; I suppose so.

JULIA. And you know how to tell about them. And you've such an engaging way about you . . . nobody could help but take to you.

JACK. Cut out the taffy. Who's your friend?

JULIA. Her name's Hegan.

JACK. A woman?

JULIA. A girl, yes. And she's coming right along, Jack. You must take a little trouble with her, for if we can only bring her through, she can do a lot for us. She's got no end of money.

JACK. No relative of Jim Hegan, I hope?

JULIA. She's his daughter.

JACK. [*With a bound.*] What!

JULIA. His only daughter.

JACK. Good God, Julia!

JULIA. What's the matter?

JACK. You know I don't want to meet people like that.

JULIA. Why not?

JACK. I don't care to mix with them. I've nothing to say to them.

JULIA. My dear Jack, the girl can't help her father.

JACK. I know that, and I'm sorry for her. But, meantime, I've got my work to do . . .

JULIA. You couldn't be doing any better work than this. If we can make a Socialist of Laura Hegan . . .

JACK. Oh, stuff, Julia! I've given up chasing after will-o'-the-wisps like that.

JULIA. But think what she could do!

JACK. Yes. I used to think what a whole lot of people could do. You might as well ask me to think what her father could do . . . if he only wanted to do it, instead of poisoning the life-blood of the city, and piling up his dirty millions. Go about this town and see the misery and horror . . . and think that it's Jim Hegan who sits at the top and reaps the profit of it all! It's Jim Hegan who is back of the organization . . . he's the real power behind Boss Grimes. It's he who puts up the money and makes possible this whole régime of vice and graft . . .

JULIA. My dear boy, don't be silly.

JACK. How do you mean? Isn't it true?

JULIA. Of course it's true . . . but why declaim to me about it? You forget you are talking to the champion female muckraker of the country.

JACK. Yes, that's right. But I don't want to meet these people socially. They mean well, a lot of them, I suppose; but they've been accustomed all their lives to being people of importance . . . to have everybody stand in awe of them, because of their stolen money, and all the wonderful things they might do with it if they only would.

JULIA. My dear Jack, did you ever observe anything of the tuft-hunter in me?

JACK. No, I don't know that I have. But it's never too late.

JULIA. [Laughing.] Well, until you do, have a little faith in me! Meet Laura Hegan, and judge for yourself.

JACK. [Grumbling.] All right, I'll meet her. But let me tell you, I don't propose to spare her feelings. She'll get things straight from me.

JULIA. That's all right, my boy. Give her the class war and the Revolution with a capital R! Tell her you're the only original representative of the disinherited proletariat, and that some day, before long, you intend to plant the red flag over her daddy's palace. [Seriously.] Of course, what you'll actually do is meet her like a gentleman, and tell her of some of your adventures in Russia, and give her some idea of what's going on outside of her little Fifth avenue set.

JACK. Where did you run on to her?

JULIA. I met her at the settlement.

JACK. Good Lord! Jim Hegan's daughter! [Laughs.] They were toadying to her there, I'll wager.

JULIA. Well, you know what settlement people are.

She's been coming there for quite a while, and seems to be interested. She's given them quite a lot of money.

JACK. No doubt.

JULIA. I had a little talk with her one afternoon. She's a quiet, self-contained girl, but she gave me a peculiar impression. She seemed to be unhappy; there was a kind of troubled note in what she said. I had felt uncomfortable about meeting her . . . you can imagine, after my study of "Tammany and the Traction Trust."

JACK. Did she mention that?

JULIA. No, she never has. But I've several times had the feeling that she was trying to get up the courage to do it. I've thought, somehow, that she must be suffering about her father.

JACK. My God! Wouldn't it be a joke if Nemesis were to get at Jim Hegan through his daughter?

JULIA. Yes; wouldn't it!

JACK. How do you suppose he takes her reform activities?

JULIA. I don't know, but I fancy they must have had it out. She's not the sort of person to let herself be turned back when her mind's made up.

JACK. A sort of chip of the old block. [*After a pause.*] If I'd known what was up, I wouldn't have suggested asking anybody else to come . . .

JULIA. Oh, that's all right; it won't make any difference.

JACK. This chap, Montague, that I 'phoned to you about . . . he's a sort of a convert of my own.

JULIA. I see. We'll reciprocate.

JACK. I think I've got Montague pretty well landed. You'll be interested in him . . . it's quite a story. It was last election day. . .

The bell rings.

JULIA. Ah, there's somebody. [*She goes to the door; calls.*] Is that you, Miss Hegan?

LAURA. [*Off.*] Yes, it's I.

JULIA. You found your way, did you?

LAURA. Oh, no trouble at all. [*Enters, a tall, stately girl, about twenty-three; simply but elegantly clad.*] How do you do?

JULIA. I am so glad to see you. Jack, this is Miss Hegan. Mr. Bullen.

LAURA. How do you do, Mr. Bullen?

JACK. I am very glad to meet you, Miss Hegan.

JULIA. Let me take your things.

LAURA. [*Looking about.*] Oh, what a cozy place! I think these model tenements are delightful.

JULIA. They're indispensable to us agitators . . . an oasis in a desert.

JACK. Built for the proletariat, and inhabited by cranks.

LAURA. Is that the truth?

JULIA. It's certainly the truth about this one. Below me are two painters and a settlement worker, and next door is a blind Anarchist and a Yiddish poet.

LAURA. What's the reason for it?

JULIA. [*Going to room off left with* LAURA'S *things.*] The places are clean and cheap; and whenever the poor can't pay their rent, we take their homes.

JACK. The elimination of the unfit.

LAURA. It sounds like a tragic explanation; but I guess it's true. [*Looking at Jack.*] And so this is Mr. Bullen. For such a famous revolutionist, I expected to find some one more dangerous-looking.

JULIA. [*Returning.*] Don't make up your mind too soon about Jack. He's liable to startle you.

LAURA. I'm not easily startled any more. I'm getting quite used to meeting revolutionists.

JACK. You don't call them revolutionists that you meet at the settlement, I hope?

LAURA. No; but all sorts of people come there.

JULIA. By the way, Jack 'phoned me this afternoon, and said he'd invited a friend here. I hope you don't mind.

LAURA. Why, no; not at all. Is it one of your Russian friends?

JACK. Oh, no; he's an American. His name is Montague. I was just starting to tell Julia about him when you came in.

LAURA. Go ahead.

JACK. It was quite an adventure. I don't know that I've ever had one that was more exciting. And I've had quite some, you know.

LAURA. Yes; I've been told so.

JACK. It was last election day, in a polling place on the Bowery. I was a watcher for the Socialists, and this Montague was one of the watchers for the reform crowd. The other one was drunk, and so he had the work all to himself. It was in the heart of Leary's district, and the crowd there was a tough one, I can tell you. It was a close election.

LAURA. Yes; I know.

JACK. There'd been all kinds of monkey-work going on, and the box was full of marked and defective ballots, and Montague set to work to make them throw them out. I didn't pay much attention at first. I was only there to see that our own ballots were counted; but pretty soon I began to take interest. He had every one in the place against him. There was a Tammany inspector of elections and four tally clerks . . . all in with Tammany, of course. There were three or four Tammany policemen, and, outside of the railing, the worst crowd of toughs that ever you laid eyes on. To make matters worse, there were several men inside who had no business to be there . . . one of them a Judge of the City Court, and another a State's attorney . . . and all of them storming at Montague.

JULIA. What did he do?

JACK. He just made them throw out the marked ballots. They were willing enough to put them to one side, but wanted to count them in on the tally sheets. And, of course, Montague knew perfectly well that if they ever counted them in they'd close up at the end, and that would be all there was to it. He had the law with him, of course. He's a lawyer himself, and he seemed to know it all by heart; and he'd quote it to them, paragraph by paragraph, and they'd look it up and find that he was right, and, of course, that only made them madder. The old Judge would start up in his seat. "Officer!" he'd shout (he was a red-faced, ignorant fellow . . . a typical barroom politician, "I demand that you put that man out of here." And the cop actually laid his hand on Montague's shoulder; if he'd ever been landed on the other side of that railing the crowd would have torn him to pieces. But the man stayed as cool as a cucumber. "Officer," he said, "you are aware that I am an election official, here under the protection of the law; and if you refuse me that protection you are liable to a sentence in State's prison." Then he'd quote another paragraph.

JULIA. It's a wonder he ever held them.

JACK. He did it; he made them throw out forty-seven ballots . . . and thirty-eight of them were Tammany ballots, too. There was one time when I thought the gang was going to break loose, and I sneaked out and telephoned for help. Then I came back and spoke up for him. I wanted them to know there'd be one witness.

You should have seen the grateful look that Montague gave me.

LAURA. I can imagine it.

JULIA. And how did it end?

JACK. Why, you see, we kept them there till eleven o'clock at night, and by that time everybody knew that Tammany had won, and the ballots were not needed. So the old Judge patted us on the back and told us we were heroes, and invited us out to get drunk with him. Montague and I walked home together through the election din, and got acquainted. I don't know that I ever met a man I took to more quickly.

LAURA. You are making a Socialist out of him, of course?

JACK. Oh, he's coming on. But he is not the sort of man to take his ideas from any one else . . . he wants to see for himself. He hasn't been in New York long, you know . . . he comes from the South . . . from Mississippi.

LAURA. [*Startled.*] From Mississippi! What's his first name?

JACK. Allan.

LAURA. [*Betraying emotion.*] Allan Montague!

JACK. Do you know him?

LAURA. Yes; I know him very well, indeed. Oh . . . I didn't . . . that is . . . I have not seen him for a long time. [*Recovering her poise.*] Is he surely coming?

JACK. He generally keeps his engagements.

JULIA. How did you come to know him?

LAURA. He's Ollie Montague's brother.

JACK. Who's Ollie Montague?

LAURA. He's one of those pretty boys that everybody knows in society; he brought his brother up from the South to introduce him. He was in some business deal or other with my father. Then he seemed to drop out of everything, and nobody sees him any more. I don't know why.

JACK. I think he was disgusted with his experiences.

LAURA. Oh!

JACK. [*Realizing that he had said something awkward.*] I think I was the first Socialist he'd ever met. He had just gotten to the stage of despair. He'd started out with a long program of reforms . . . and he was going to educate the people to them . . . one by one, until he'd made them all effective. I said to him: "By the time you've got the attention of the public on reform number thirty . . . what do you suppose the politicians will have been doing with reform number one?"

JULIA. We all have to go through that stage. I can remember just as well . . . [*A ring upon the bell.*] Ah, there he is.

JACK. [*Rises and goes to the door.*] But I think he's most through butting his head against the stone wall! [*Calls.*] Are you there, old man?

MONTAGUE. [*Off.*] I'm here!

JACK. How are you?

MONTAGUE. Fine!

JACK. Come right in.

MONTAGUE. [*Enters; a tall, handsome man of thirty; self-contained and slow of speech; the dark type of a Southerner.*] I'm a trifle late. [*Sees* LAURA; *starts.*] Miss Hegan! You! [*Recovers himself.*] Why . . . an unexpected pleasure!

LAURA. Unexpected on both sides, Mr. Montague.

MONTAGUE. I'm delighted to meet you, really!

They shake hands.

JACK. Julia, my friend, Mr. Montague. Miss Patterson.

MONTAGUE. I'm very glad to meet you, Miss Patterson.

JULIA. We had no idea we were bringing old friends together.

MONTAGUE. No; it was certainly a coincidence.

LAURA. It's been . . . let me see . . . a year since we've met.

MONTAGUE. It must be fully that.

LAURA. Where do you keep yourself these days?

MONTAGUE. Oh, I'm studying, in a quiet way.

LAURA. And none of your old friends ever see you?

MONTAGUE. I don't get about much.

LAURA. [*Earnestly.*] And friendship means so little to you as that?

MONTAGUE. I . . . it would be hard to explain. I have been busy with politics . . .

A pause of embarrassment.

JULIA. Mr. Bullen has just been telling us about your heroism.

MONTAGUE. My heroism? Where?

JULIA. At the polling place.

MONTAGUE. Oh, that! It was nothing.

LAURA. It seemed like a good deal to us.

MONTAGUE. Make him tell you about some of his own adventures.

JULIA. Would you ever think, to look at his innocent countenance, that he had helped to hold a building for six hours against Russian artillery?

LAURA. Good heavens! Where was this?

JULIA. During the St. Petersburg uprising.

LAURA. And weren't you frightened to death?

JACK. [*Laughing.*] No; we were too busy taking potshots at the Cossacks. It was like the hunting season in the Adirondacks.

LAURA. And how did it turn out?

JACK. Oh, they were too much for us in the end. I got away, across the ice of the Neva . . . I had the heel of one shoe shot off. And yet people tell us romance is dead! Anybody who is looking for romance, and knows what it is, can find all he wants in Russia.

Pause.

LAURA. [*To* MONTAGUE.] Have you seen my father lately?

MONTAGUE. No; not for some time.

LAURA. You may see him this evening. He promised to call for me.

MONTAGUE. Indeed!

JACK. Oh, by the way, Julia, I forgot! How's Annie?

LAURA. Oh, yes; how is she?

JULIA. She's doing well, I think. Better every day.

LAURA. Is she still violent?

JULIA. Not so much. I can always handle her now.

LAURA. Is she in the next room?

Looking to the right.

JULIA. Yes. She's been asleep since afternoon.

LAURA. And you still won't let me send her to a hospital?

JULIA. Oh, no. Truly, it would kill the poor girl.

LAURA. But you . . . with all your work, and your engagements?

JULIA. She's very quiet. And the neighbors come in and help when I'm out. They all sympathize.

LAURA. Talking about heroism . . . it seems to me that you are entitled to mention.

JULIA. Why, nonsense! . . . the girl was simply thrown into my arms.

LAURA. Most people would have managed to step out of the way, just the same. You've heard the story, have you, Mr. Montague?

MONTAGUE. Bullen has told it to me. You haven't been able to get any justice?

JACK. From the police? Hardly! But we're keeping

at it, to make the story complete. I went to see Captain Quinn to-day. "What's this?" says he. "Annie Rogers again? Didn't your lady frien' get her pitcher in the papers over that case? An' what more does she want?"

JULIA. I went this afternoon to see the Tammany leader of our district . . .

MONTAGUE. Leary?

JULIA. The same. I went straight into his saloon. "Lady," says he, "the goil's nutty! You got a bughouse patient on your hands! This here talk about the white-slave traffic, ma'am . . . it's all the work o' these magazine muckrakers!" "Meaning myself, Mr Leary?" said I, and he looked kind of puzzled. I don't think he knew who I was.

MONTAGUE. All the work of the muckrakers! I see Boss Grimes is out to that effect also.

JACK. And I see that half a dozen clergymen sat down to a public banquet with him the other day. That's what we've come to in New York! Bob Grimes, with his hands on every string of the whole infamous system . . . with his paws in every filthy graft-pot in the city! Bob Grimes, the type and symbol of it all! Every time I see a picture of that bulldog face, it seems to me as if I were confronting all the horrors that I've ever fought in my life!

JULIA. It's curious to note how much less denunciation of Tammany one hears now than in the old days.

MONTAGUE. Tammany's getting respectable.

JACK. The big interests have found out how to use it. The traction gang, especially . . .

He stops abruptly; a tense pause.

LAURA. [*Leaning toward him, with great earnestness.*] Mr. Bullen, is that really true?

JACK. That is true, Miss Hegan.

LAURA. Mr. Bullen, you will understand what it means

to me to hear that statement made. I hear it made continually, and I ask if it is true, and I am told that it is a slander. How am I to know? [*A pause.*] Would you be able to tell me that you know it of your own personal knowledge?

JACK. [*Weighing the words.*] No; I could not say that.

LAURA. Would you say that you could prove it to a jury?

JACK. I would say, that if I had to prove it, I could get the evidence.

LAURA. What would you say, Mr. Montague?

MONTAGUE. I would rather not say, Miss Hegan.

LAURA. Please! Please! I want you to answer me.

MONTAGUE. [*After a pause.*] I would say that I shall be able to prove it very shortly.

LAURA. How do you mean?

MONTAGUE. I have been giving most of my time to a study of just that question, and I think that I shall have the evidence.

LAURA. I see.

She sinks back, very white; a pause; the bell rings.

JULIA. Who can that be?

JACK. [*Springing up.*] Let me answer it. [*Presses button; then, to* MONTAGUE.] I had no idea you were going in for that, old man.

MONTAGUE. This is the first time I have ever mentioned it to any one.

JULIA. [*Rising, hoping to relieve an embarrassing situation.*] I hope this isn't any more company.

JACK. [*To* MONTAGUE, *aside.*] You must let me tell you a few things that I know. I've been running down a little story about Grimes and the traction crowd.

MONTAGUE. Indeed! What is it?

JACK. I can't tell it to you now . . . it would take

too long. But, gee! If I can get the evidence, it'll make your hair stand on end! It has to do with the Grand Avenue Railroad suit.

MONTAGUE. The one that's pending in the Court of Appeals?

JACK. Yes. You see, Jim Hegan stands to lose a fortune by it, and I've reason to believe that there's some monkey-work being done with the Court. It happens that one of the judges has a nephew . . . a dissipated chap, who hates him. He's an old college friend of mine, and he's trying to get some evidence for me.

MONTAGUE. Good Lord!

JACK. And think, it concerns Jim Hegan personally.

A knock at the door.

JULIA. I'll go.

Opens the door.

HEGAN. [*Without.*] Good evening. Is Miss Hegan here?

LAURA. [*Standing up.*] Father!

JULIA. Won't you come in?

HEGAN. Thank you. [*Enters; a tall, powerfully built man, with a square jaw, wide, over-arching eyebrows, and keen eyes that peer at one; a prominent nose, the aspect of the predatory eagle; a man accustomed to let other people talk and to read their thoughts.*] Why, Mr. Montague, you here?

MONTAGUE. Mr. Hegan! Why, how do you do?

LAURA. We stumbled on each other by chance. Father, this is Miss Patterson.

HEGAN. I am very pleased to meet you, Miss Patterson.

JULIA. How do you do, Mr. Hegan?

They shake hands.

LAURA. And Mr. Bullen.

BULLEN. [*Remaining where he is; stiffly.*] Good evening, Mr. Hegan.

HEGAN. Good evening, sir. [*Turns to* LAURA.] My dear, I finished up downtown sooner than I expected, and I have another conference at the house. I stopped on to see if you cared to come now, or if I should send back the car for you.

LAURA. I think you'd best send it back.

JULIA. Why, yes . . . she only just got here.

HEGAN. Very well.

JULIA. Won't you stop a minute?

HEGAN. No. I really can't. Mr. Grimes is waiting for me downstairs.

LAURA. [*Involuntarily.*] Mr. Grimes!

HEGAN. Yes.

LAURA. Robert Grimes?

HEGAN. [*Surprised.*] Yes. Why?

LAURA. Nothing; only we happened to be just talking about him.

HEGAN. I see.

JACK. [*Aggressively.*] We happen to have one of his victims in the next room.

HEGAN. [*Perplexed.*] One of his victims?

JULIA. [*Protesting.*] Jack!

JACK. A daughter of the slums. One of the helpless girls who have to pay the tribute that he . . .

A piercing and terrifying scream is heard off right.

JULIA. Annie!

Runs off.

HEGAN. What's that?

The screams continue.

JULIA. [*Off.*] Help! Help!

Jack, who is nearest, leaps toward the door; but, before he can reach it, it is flung violently open.

ANNIE. [*Enters, delirious, her bare arms and throat*

covered with bruises, her hair loose, and her aspect wild: an Irish peasant girl, aged twenty.] No! No! Let me go!

  Rushes into the opposite corner, and cowers in terror.

JULIA. [*Following her.*] Annie! Annie!

ANNIE. [*Flings her off, and stretches out her arms.*] What do you want with me? Help! Help! I won't do it! I won't stay! Let me alone!

  Wild and frantic sobbing.

JULIA. Annie, dear! Annie! Look at me! Don't you know me? I'm Julia! Your own Julia! No one shall hurt you . . . no one!

ANNIE. [*Stares at her wildly.*] He's after me still! He'll follow me here! He won't let me get away from him! Oh, save me!

JULIA. [*Embracing her.*] Listen to me, dear Don't think of things like that. You are in my home . . . nothing can hurt you. Don't let these evil dreams take hold of you.

ANNIE. [*Stares, as if coming out of a trance.*] Why didn't you help me before?

JULIA. Come, dear . . . come.

ANNIE. It's too late . . . too late! Oh . . . I can't forget about it!

JULIA. Yes, dear. I know . . .

ANNIE. [*Seeing the others.*] Who? . . .

JULIA. They are all friends; they will help you. Come, dear . . . lie down again.

ANNIE. Oh, what shall I do?

  Is led off, sobbing.

JULIA. It will be all right, dear.

  Exit; a pause.

HEGAN. What does this mean?

JACK. [*Promptly and ruthlessly.*] It means that you have been seeing the white-slave traffic in action.

HEGAN. I don't understand.

JACK. [*Quietly, but with suppressed passion.*] Tens of thousands of girl slaves are needed for the markets of our great cities . . . for the lumber camps of the North, the mining camps of the West, the ditches of Panama. And every four or five years the supply must be renewed, and so the business of gathering these girl-slaves from our slums is one of the great industries of the city. This girl, Annie Rogers, a decent girl from the North of Ireland, was lured into a dance hall and drugged, and then taken to a brothel and locked in a third-story room. They took her clothing away from her, but she broke down her door at night and fled to the street in her wrapper and flung herself into Miss Patterson's arms. Two men were pursuing her . . . they tried to carry her off. Miss Patterson called a policeman . . . but he said the girl was insane. Only by making a disturbance and drawing a crowd was my friend able to save her. And now, we have been the rounds . . from the sergeant at the station, and the police captain, to the Chief of Police and the Mayor himself; we have been to the Tammany leader of the district . . . the real boss of the neighborhood . . . and there is no justice to be had anywhere for Annie Rogers!

HEGAN. Impossible!

JACK. You have my word for it, sir. And the reason for it is that this hideous traffic is one of the main cogs in our political machine. The pimps and the panders, the cadets and *maquereaux* . . . they vote the ticket of the organization; they contribute to the campaign funds; they serve as colonizers and repeaters at the polls. The tribute that they pay amounts to millions; and it is shared from the lowest to the highest in the organization . . . from the ward man on the street and the police captain, up to the inner circle of the chiefs of Tammany Hall . . . yes, even to your friend, Mr. Robert Grimes, himself! A thousand times, sir, has the truth about this monstrous infamy been put before the people of your city; and that they have not long ago risen in their wrath and driven its agents from their midst is due to but one single fact . . . that this infamous organization of crime and graft is backed at each election time by the millions of the great public service corporations. It is they . . .

MONTAGUE. [*Interfering.*] Bullen!

JACK. Let me go on! It is they, sir, who finance the thugs and repeaters who desecrate our polls. It is they who suborn our press and blind the eyes of our people. It is they who are responsible for this traffic in the flesh of our women. It is they who have to answer for the tottering reason of that poor peasant girl in the next room!

LAURA. [*Has been listening to this speech, white with horror; as the indictment proceeds, she covers her face with her hands; at this point she breaks into uncontrollable weeping.*] Oh! I can't stand it!

HEGAN. [*Springing to her side.*] My dear!

LAURA. [*Clasping him.*] Father! Father!

HEGAN. My child! I have begged you not to come to these places! Why should you see such things?

LAURA. [*Wildly.*] Why should I not see them, so long as they exist?

HEGAN. [*Angrily.*] I won't have it. This is the end of it! I mean what I say! Come home with me! . . . Come home at once!

LAURA. With Grimes? I won't meet that man!

HEGAN. Very well, then. You need not meet him. I'll call a cab, and take you myself. Where are your things?

LAURA. [*Looking to the left.*] In that room.
HEGAN. Come, then.
   Takes her off.
JACK. [*Turns to* MONTAGUE, *and to* JULIA, *who appears in doorway at right.*] We gave it to them straight that time, all right!

CURTAIN

ACT II

Library of "The Towers," HEGAN'S *Long Island country place. A spacious room, furnished luxuriously, but with good taste. A large table, with lamp and books in the centre, and easy-chairs beside it Up stage are French windows leading to a veranda, with drive below; a writing desk between the windows. Entrance right and left. A telephone stand left, and a clock on wall right.*

At rise: ANDREWS, *standing by the table, opening some letters.*

LAURA. [*Enters from veranda.*] Good afternoon, Mr. Andrews.

ANDREWS. Good afternoon, Miss Hegan.

LAURA. Has father come yet?

ANDREWS. No; he said he'd be back about five.

LAURA. Is he surely coming?

ANDREWS. Oh, yes. He has an important engagement here.

LAURA. He's working very hard these days.

ANDREWS. He has a good deal on his mind just now.

LAURA. It's this Grand Avenue Railroad business.

ANDREWS. Yes. If it should go against him, it would confuse his plans very much.

LAURA. Is the matter never going to be decided?

ANDREWS. We're expecting the decision any day now. That's why he's so much concerned. He has to hold the market, you see . . .

LAURA. The decision's liable to affect the market?
ANDREWS. Oh, yes . . . very much, indeed.
LAURA. I see. And then . . .

'Phone rings.

ANDREWS. Excuse me. Hello! Yes, this is Mr. Hegan's place. Mr. Montague? Why, yes; I believe he's to be here this afternoon. Yes . . . wait a moment . . . [*To* LAURA.] It's some one asking for Mr. Montague.

LAURA. Who is it?

ANDREWS. Hello! Who is this, please? [*To* LAURA.] It's Mr. Bullen.

LAURA. Mr. Bullen? I'll speak to him. [*Takes 'phone.*] Hello, Mr. Bullen! This is Miss Hegan. I'm glad to hear from you. How are you? Why, yes, Mr. Montague is coming out . . . I expect him here any time. He was to take the three-five . . . just a moment. [*Looks at clock.*] If the train's on time, he's due here now. We sent to meet him. Call up again in about five minutes. Oh, you have to see him? As soon as that? Nothing wrong, I hope. Well, he couldn't get back to the city until after six. Oh, then you're right near us. Why don't you come over? . . . That's the quickest way. No; take the trolley and come right across. I'll be delighted to see you. What's that? Why, Mr. Bullen! How perfectly preposterous! My father doesn't blame you for what happened. Don't think of it. Come right along. I'll take it ill of you if you don't . . . truly I will. Yes; please do. You'll just have time to get the next trolley. Get off at the Merrick road, and I'll see there's an auto there to meet you. Very well. Good-bye. [*To* ANDREWS.] Mr. Andrews, will you see there's a car sent down to the trolley to meet Mr. Bullen?

ANDREWS. All right.

Exit.

LAURA. [*Stands by table, in deep thought, takes a*

note from table and studies it; shakes her head.] He didn't want to come. He doesn't want to talk to me. But he must! Ah, there he is. [*Sound of a motor heard. She waits, then goes to the window.*] Ah, Mr. Montague!

MONTAGUE. [*Enters centre.*] Good afternoon, Miss Hegan.

LAURA. You managed to catch the train, I see.

MONTAGUE. Yes. I just did.

LAURA. It is so good of you to come.

MONTAGUE. Not at all. I am glad to be here.

LAURA. I just had a telephone call from Mr. Bullen.

MONTAGUE. [*Starting.*] From Bullen?

LAURA. Yes. He said he had to see you about something.

MONTAGUE. [*Eagerly.*] Where was he?

LAURA. He was at his brother's place. I told him to come here.

MONTAGUE. Oh! Is he coming?

LAURA. Yes; he'll be here soon.

MONTAGUE. Thank you very much.

LAURA. He said it was something quite urgent.

MONTAGUE. Yes. He has some important papers for me.

LAURA. I see he made a speech last night that stirred up the press.

MONTAGUE. [*Smiling.*] Yes.

LAURA. He is surely a tireless fighter.

MONTAGUE. It's such men as Bullen who keep the world moving.

LAURA. And do you agree with him, Mr. Montague?

MONTAGUE. In what way?

LAURA. That the end of it all is to be a revolution.

MONTAGUE. I don't know, Miss Hegan. I find I am moving that way. I used to think we could control capital. Now I am beginning to suspect that it is in the nature of capital to have its way, and that if the people wish to rule they must own the capital.

LAURA. [*After a pause.*] Mr. Montague, I had to ask you to come out and see me, because I'd promised my father I would not go into the city again for a while. I've not been altogether well since that evening at Julia's.

MONTAGUE. I am sorry to hear that, Miss Hegan.

LAURA. It's nothing, but it worries my father, you know. [*A pause.*] I thought we should be alone this afternoon, but I find that my father is coming out . . . and Mr. Bullen is coming also. So I mayn't have time to say all I wished to say to you. But I must thank you for coming.

MONTAGUE. I was very glad to come, Miss Hegan.

LAURA. I can appreciate your embarrassment at being asked to . . .

MONTAGUE. No!

LAURA. We must deal frankly with each other. I know that you did not want to come. I know that you have tried to put an end to our friendship.

MONTAGUE. [*Hesitates.*] Miss Hegan, let me explain my position.

LAURA. I think I understand it already. You have found evil conditions which you wish to oppose, and you were afraid that our friendship might stand in the way.

MONTAGUE. [*In a low voice.*] Miss Hegan, I came to New York an entire stranger two years ago, and my brother introduced me to his rich friends. By one of them I was asked to take charge of a law case. It was a case of very great importance, which served to give me an opening into the inner life of the city. I discovered that, in their blind struggle for power, our great capitalists had lost all sense of the difference between honesty and crime. I found that trust funds were being abused . . . that courts and legislatures were being corrupted . . . the very financial stability of the country was being wrecked. The thing shocked me to the bottom of my soul, and I set to work to give the public some light on the situation. Then, what happened, Miss Hegan? My newly made rich friends cut me dead; they began to circulate vile slanders about me . . . they insulted me openly, on more than one occasion. So, don't you see?

LAURA. Yes, I see. But could you not have trusted a friendship such as ours?

MONTAGUE. I did not dare.

LAURA. You saw that you had to fight my father, and you thought that I would blindly take his side.

MONTAGUE. [*Hesitating.*] I . . . I couldn't suppose . . .

LAURA. Listen. You have told me your situation; now, imagine mine. Imagine a girl brought up in luxury, with a father whom she loves very dearly, and who loves her more than any one else in the world. Everything is done to make her happy . . . to keep her contented and peaceful. But as she grows up, she reads and listens . . . and, little by little, it dawns upon her that her father is one of the leaders in this terrible struggle that you have spoken of. She hears about wrongdoing; she is told that her father's enemies have slandered him. At first, perhaps, she believes that. But time goes on . . . she sees suffering and oppression . . . she begins to realize a little of cause and effect. She wants to help, she wants to do right, but there is no way for her to know. She goes to one person after another, and no one will deal frankly with her. No one will tell her the truth . . . absolutely no one! [*Leaning forward with intensity.*] No one! No one!

MONTAGUE. I see.

LAURA. So it was with you . . . and with our friendship. I knew that you had broken it off for such reasons. I knew that there was nothing personal . . . it was nothing that I had done . . .

MONTAGUE. No! Surely not!

LAURA. [*Gazes about nervously.*] And then . . . the other night . . . you told me you were investigating the traction companies of New York . . . their connection with politics, and so on. Ever since then I have felt that you were the one person I must talk with. Don't you see?

MONTAGUE. Yes; I see.

LAURA. I have sought for some one who will tell me the truth. Will you?

MONTAGUE. [*In a low voice.*] You must realize what you are asking of me, Miss Hegan.

LAURA. I have not brought you here without realizing that. You must help me!

MONTAGUE. Very well. I will do what I can.

LAURA. [*Leaning forward.*] I wish to know about my father. I wish to know to what extent he is involved in these evils that you speak of.

MONTAGUE. Your father is in the game, and he has played it the way the game is played.

LAURA. Has he been better than the others, or worse?

MONTAGUE. About the same, Miss Hegan.

LAURA. He has been more successful than they.

MONTAGUE. He has been very successful.

LAURA. You were concerned in some important deal with my father, were you not?

MONTAGUE. I was.

LAURA. Then you withdrew. Was that because there was something wrong in it?

MONTAGUE. It was, Miss Hegan.

LAURA. There were corrupt things done?

ACT II] THE MACHINE 99

MONTAGUE. There were many kinds of corrupt things done.

LAURA. And was my father responsible for them?

MONTAGUE. Yes.

LAURA. Directly?

MONTAGUE. Yes; directly.

LAURA. Then my father is a bad man?

MONTAGUE. [*After a pause.*] Your father finds himself in the midst of an evil system. He is the victim of conditions which he did not create.

LAURA. Ah, now you are trying to spare me!

MONTAGUE. No. I should say that to any one. I am at war with the system . . . not with individuals. It is the old story of hating the sin and loving the sinner. Your father's rivals are just as reckless as he . . . take Murdock, for instance, the man who is behind this Grand Avenue Railroad matter. It is hard for a woman to understand that situation.

LAURA. I can understand some things very clearly. I go down into the slums and I see all that welter of misery I see the forces of evil that exist there, defiant and hateful . . . the saloons and the gambling-houses, and that ghastly white-slave traffic, of which Annie Rogers is the victim. And there is the political organization, taking its toll from all these, and using it to keep itself in power. And there is Boss Grimes, who is at the head of all . . . and he is one of my father's intimate associates. I ask about it, and I am told that it is a matter of "business." But why should my father do business with a man whose chief source of income is vice?

MONTAGUE. That is not quite the case, Miss Hegan.

LAURA. Doesn't the vice tribute go to him?

MONTAGUE. Part of it does, I have no doubt. But it would be a very small part of his income.

LAURA. What then?

MONTAGUE. The vice graft serves for the police and the district leaders and the little men; what really pays nowadays is what has come to be called "honest graft."

LAURA. What is that?

MONTAGUE. The business deals that are made with the public service corporations.

LAURA. Ah! That is what I wish to know about!

MONTAGUE. For instance, I am running a street railway . . .

LAURA. [*Quickly.*] My father is running them all!

MONTAGUE. Very well. Your father is in alliance with the organization; he is given franchises and public privileges for practically nothing; and in return he gives the contracts for constructing the subways and street-car lines to companies organized by the politicians. These companies are simply paper companies . . . they farm out the contracts to the real builders, skimming off a profit of twenty or thirty per cent. One of these companies received contracts last year to the value of thirty million dollars.

LAURA. And so that is how Grimes gets his money?

MONTAGUE. Grimes' brother is the president of the company I have reference to.

LAURA. I see; it is a regular system.

MONTAGUE. It is a business, and there is no way to punish it . . . it does not violate any law . . .

LAURA. And yet it is quite as bad!

MONTAGUE. It is far worse, because of its vast scope. It carries every form of corruption in its train. It means the prostitution of our whole system of government . . . the subsidizing of our newspapers, and of the great political parties. It means that judges are chosen who will decide in favor of the corporations; that legislators are nominated who will protect them against attack. It means everywhere the enthronement of ignorance and incompetence, of injustice and fraud.

LAURA. And in the end the public pays for it?

MONTAGUE. In the end the public pays for everything. The stolen franchises are unloaded on the market for ten times what they cost, and the people pay their nickels for a wretched, broken-down service. They pay for it in the form of rent and taxes for a dishonest administration. Every struggling unfortunate in the city pays for it, when he comes into contact with the system . . . when he seeks for help, or even for justice. It was that side of it that shocked me most of all . . . I being a lawyer, you see. The corrupting of our courts . . .

LAURA. The judges are bought, Mr. Montague?

MONTAGUE. The judges are selected, Miss Hegan.

LAURA. Selected! I see.

MONTAGUE. And that system prevails from the Supreme Court of the State down to the petty Police Magistrates, before whom the poor come to plead.

LAURA. And that is why the white-slave traffic goes unpunished!

MONTAGUE. That is why.

LAURA. And why no one would move a hand for Annie Rogers!

MONTAGUE. That is why.

LAURA. And my father is responsible for it!

MONTAGUE. [*Gravely.*] Yes; I think he is, Miss Hegan.

A pause.

LAURA. Have you seen Julia Patterson lately?

MONTAGUE. I saw her last night.

LAURA. And how is Annie?

MONTAGUE. She . . . [*Hesitates.*] She is dead.

LAURA. [*Starting.*] Oh!

MONTAGUE. She died the night before last.

LAURA. [*Stares at him, then gives a wild start, and cries*] She . . . she . . .

MONTAGUE. She killed herself.

LAURA. Oh!

MONTAGUE. She cut her throat.

LAURA. [*Hides her face and sinks against the table, shuddering and overcome.*] Oh, the poor girl! The poor, poor girl! [*Suddenly she springs up.*] Can't you see? Can't you see? It is things like that that are driving me to distraction!

MONTAGUE. [*Starting toward her.*] Miss Hegan . . .

LAURA. [*Covering her face again.*] Oh! oh! It is horrible! I can't stand it! I . . .

Sound of motor heard; they listen.

LAURA. That is my father's car . . . Mr. Montague, will you excuse me? I must have a talk with my father . . .

MONTAGUE. Certainly. Let me go away . . .

LAURA. No; please wait. Just take a little stroll. I . . .

MONTAGUE. Certainly, I understand.

Exit right.

LAURA. [*Seeks to compose herself; then goes to window.*] Father!

HEGAN. [*Off.*] Yes, dear.

LAURA. Come here.

HEGAN. [*Enters.*] What is it?

LAURA. Father, I have just had dreadful news . .

HEGAN. What?

LAURA. Annie Rogers . . . that poor girl, you know . . .

HEGAN. Yes.

LAURA. She has killed herself.

HEGAN. No!

LAURA. She cut her own throat.

HEGAN. Oh, my dear! [*Starts toward her.*] I am so sorry . . .

LAURA. [*Quickly.*] No, father! Listen! You must talk to me . . . you must talk to me this time!

HEGAN. My child . . .

LAURA. You cannot put me off. You cannot, I tell you!

HEGAN. Laura, dear, you are upset . . .

LAURA. No! That is not so! I have perfect control of myself. There is no use crying . . . the girl is dead. That can't be helped. But I mean to understand about it. I mean to know who is responsible for her death.

HEGAN. My dear, these evils are hard to know of . . .

LAURA. That house to which that girl was taken . . . there is a law against such places, is there not?

HEGAN. Yes, my dear.

LAURA. And why is not the law enforced?

HEGAN. It has not been found possible to enforce such laws.

LAURA. But why not?

HEGAN. Why, my dear, this evil . . .

LAURA. These people pay money to the police, do they not?

HEGAN. Why, yes; I imagine . . .

LAURA. Don't tell me what you imagine . . . tell me what you know! They pay money to the police, don't they?

HEGAN. Yes.

LAURA. Then why should the police not be punished? Do those who control the police get some of the money?

HEGAN. Some of them, my dear

LAURA. That is, the leaders of Tammany

HEGAN. Possibly . . . yes.

LAURA. And Mr. Grimes . . . he gets some of it?

HEGAN. Why, my dear . . .

LAURA. Tell me!

HEGAN. But really, Laura, I never asked him what he gets.

LAURA. [*With intensity.*] Father, you must understand me! I will not be trifled with . . . I am in desperate earnest! I am determined to get to the bottom of this thing! I am no longer a child, and you must not try to deceive me! Mr. Grimes must get some of that money!

HEGAN. I think it possible, my dear.

LAURA. And do you get any?

HEGAN. Good God, Laura!

LAURA. Then what is the nature of your relationship with Grimes?

HEGAN. Really, my child, this is not fair of you. I have business connections which you cannot possibly understand . . .

LAURA. I can understand everything that you are willing for me to understand! I want to know why you must have business connections with a man like Boss Grimes.

HEGAN. My dear, I think you might take your father's word in such a case. It has nothing to do with vice, I can assure you. Grimes is a business ally of mine. He is a rich man, a great power in New York . . .

LAURA. Do you help to keep him a power in New York?

HEGAN. Why, I don't know . . .

LAURA. Do you contribute to his campaign funds?

HEGAN. Why, Laura! I am a Democrat. Surely I have a right to support my party!

LAURA. [*Quickly.*] Have you ever contributed to the Republican campaign funds?

HEGAN. [*Disconcerted; laughs.*] Why . . . really . . .

LAURA. Please answer me.

HEGAN. I am a Gold Democrat, my dear.

ACT II]   THE MACHINE   105

LAURA. I see. [*She pauses.*] You put Mr. Grimes in the way of making a great deal of money, do you not?
HEGAN. I do that.
LAURA. He is interested in companies that you give contracts to?
HEGAN. Really! You seem to be informed about my affairs!
LAURA. I have taken some trouble to inform myself. Father, don't you realize what it means to corrupt the government of the city in this way?
HEGAN. Corrupt the government, my dear?
LAURA. Does not Grimes have the nominating of judges and legislators?
HEGAN. Why, yes . . . in a way . . .
LAURA. And does he not consult with you?
HEGAN. Why, my dear . . .
LAURA. Please tell me.
HEGAN. [*Realizing that he cannot make any more admissions.*] No, my dear.
LAURA. Never?
HEGAN. Absolutely never.
LAURA. He has never made any attempt to influence the courts in your favor?
HEGAN. Never.
LAURA. Not in any way, father?
HEGAN. Not in any way.
LAURA. Nor in favor of your companies?
HEGAN. No, my dear.
LAURA. You mean, you can give me your word of honor that that is the truth?
HEGAN. I can, my dear.
LAURA. And that none of your lawyers do it? Do you mean that the courts escape your influence . . .
HEGAN. [*Laughing disconcertedly.*] Really, my dear,

this is as bad as a Government investigation! I shall have to take refuge in a lapse of memory.

LAURA. [*Intensely.*] Father! Is it nothing to you that I have the blood of that poor girl on my conscience?

HEGAN. My child!

LAURA. Yes; just that! She was caught in the grip of this ruthless system; it held her fast and crushed her life out. And we maintain this system! I profit by it . . . all this luxury and power that I enjoy comes from it directly! Can't you see what I mean?

HEGAN. I see, my dear, that you are frightfully overwrought, and that you are making yourself ill. Can't you imagine what it means to me to have you acting in this way? Here I am at one of the gravest crises of my life; I am working day and night, under frightful strain . . . I have hardly slept six hours in the past three days. And here, when I get a chance for a moment's rest, you come and put me through such an ordeal! You never think of that!

LAURA. It's just what I do think of! Why must you torture yourself so? Why . . .

HEGAN. My dear, I, too, am in the grip of the system you speak of.

LAURA. But why? Why stay in it? Haven't we money enough yet?

HEGAN. I have duties by which I am bound . . . interests that I must protect. How can I . . . [*A knock.*] Come in!

ANDREWS. [*Enters.*] Here are the papers, Mr. Hegan. They must be signed now if they're to catch this mail.

HEGAN. All right.

Sits at desk up stage and writes.

LAURA. [*Stands by table, staring before her; picks up book carelessly from table.*] "Ivanhoe" . . . [*Fingers it idly and a slip of paper falls to floor. She picks it up, glances at it, then starts.*] Oh! . . . [*Reads.*] "Memo to G., two hundred thousand on Court deal.— GRIMES." Two hundred thousand on Court deal! [*Glances back at her father; then replaces slip and lays book on table.*] Father, have you read "Ivanhoe"?

HEGAN. [*Without looking up.*] I'm reading it now. Why? Do you want it?

LAURA. No; I just happened to notice it here.

HEGAN. [*Looks up sharply, watches her, then finishes writing.*] There! [*Rises; the sound of a motor heard.*] What's that?

ANDREWS. [*Near window.*] It's Mr. Grimes.

LAURA. [*Starting.*] Grimes!

HEGAN. [*To* ANDREWS.] Bring him in.

ANDREWS *exit*.

LAURA. Father! Why do you bring that man here?

HEGAN. I'll not do it again, dear. I didn't realize. He happened to be in the neighborhood . . .

LAURA. I won't meet him!

HEGAN. [*Putting his arm about her.*] Very well, dear; come away. Try to stop worrying yourself now, for the love of me . . .

Leads her off left.

ANDREWS. [*At window.*] This way, Mr. Grimes. [GRIMES *enters; a powerfully built, broad-shouldered man of about fifty, with a massive jaw, covered with a scrubby beard; the face of a bulldog; a grim, masterful man, who never speaks except when he has to. He enters and seats himself in a chair by the table.*] Will you have a cigar? [*Grimes takes a cigar, without comment, and chews on it; sits, staring in front of him.*] Mr. Hegan will be here directly, sir.

He nods, and ANDREWS *exit.* GRIMES *continues to chew and stare in front of him. He is not under the necessity of making superfluous motions.*

HEGAN. [*Enters left.*] Hello, Grimes!
GRIMES. Hello!
HEGAN. [*Betraying anxiety.*] Well?
GRIMES. It's done.
HEGAN. What?
GRIMES. It's done.
HEGAN. Good! [*Grimes nods.*] How did you manage it?
GRIMES. [*Grimly.*] I put my hand on 'em!
HEGAN. Which one? Porter? [GRIMES *nods.*] Oh, the old hypocrite! What did you offer him? Cash? [GRIMES *shakes his head slowly.*] What?
GRIMES. Discipline!
HEGAN. [*Perplexed.*] But . . . a judge!
GRIMES. When a man's once mine, he stays mine . . . no matter if it's a life job I give him.
HEGAN. But are you sure it's safe?
GRIMES. The decision comes to-morrow.
HEGAN. [*Starting.*] What?
GRIMES. To-morrow noon.
HEGAN. But how can they write the decision?
GRIMES. They'll adopt the minority opinion.
HEGAN. Oh! I see!
 Chuckles.
GRIMES. You be ready.
HEGAN. Trust me! I'll have to go in now.
GRIMES. It'll be a great killing. Old Murdock has plunged up to his neck!
HEGAN. I know! We'll lay them flat. I'll get ready. [*Rises.*] Old Porter! Think of it! When did you see him?
GRIMES. Last night.
HEGAN. I see. I'll be with you.
GRIMES. Just a moment. I'll take the money.

HEGAN. Oh, yes. Why don't you let me hold it and buy for you?

GRIMES. I'll buy for myself.

HEGAN. Very well.

Sits at desk.

GRIMES. It's two hundred thousand.

HEGAN. That's right. [*Writes a check, rises and gives it to Grimes.*] There.

GRIMES. [*Studies the check, nods, and puts it away carefully.*] When's the next train?

HEGAN. In about ten minutes. [*Rings bell.*] Andrews!

ANDREWS. [*Enters left.*] Yes, sir.

HEGAN. I'm going into town at once. Telephone orders to the house.

ANDREWS. Yes, sir. And shall I come in this evening?

HEGAN. Yes; you'd better. And telephone Mr. Isaacson and Mr. Henry Sterns to meet me at eight o'clock for an important conference at . . . let me see, where?

GRIMES. At my rooms.

HEGAN. Very good. And they're not to fail on any account. It's urgent.

ANDREWS. Yes, sir.

HEGAN *and* GRIMES *go off centre.* ANDREWS *remains sorting papers. A knock, right.*

ANDREWS. Come in!

MONTAGUE *enters.*

ANDREWS. Oh, good afternoon. I was looking for you, Mr. Montague. Mr. Bullen has come.

MONTAGUE. Oh! Where is he?

ANDREWS. He's waiting. I'll tell him you're here. *Exit right.*

MONTAGUE. [*Stands at window and sees motor departing.*] Grimes! I wonder what that means? [*Turns away.*] And what a coincidence, that I should be here! Humph! Well, it's not my doings. Ah! Bullen!

JACK. [*Enters, right, in great excitement.*] Montague!

MONTAGUE. Yes.

JACK. I've got 'em!

MONTAGUE. What?

JACK. I've got 'em!

MONTAGUE. You don't mean it!

JACK. Got 'em dead! Got everything! There's never been a case like it!

MONTAGUE. [*Gazing about.*] Ssh! Where was it?

JACK. At Judge Porter's house.

MONTAGUE. What?

JACK. Yes. . . . Grimes came there.

MONTAGUE. When?

JACK. Last night. My friend was in the next room . . . he heard everything!

MONTAGUE. And what are they going to do?

JACK. Porter is to switch over, and sign the minority opinion, and that's to come out as the decision of the Court.

MONTAGUE. Good God! When?

JACK. To-morrow.

MONTAGUE. Impossible!

JACK. There's to be a meeting of the judges this afternoon. See . . . here's the decision! [*Takes paper from pocket.*] The one they mean to kill!

MONTAGUE. [*Looks at paper.*] Merciful heavens!

JACK. And look here! [*Unfolds a paper, which has pasted on it bits of a torn and charred note.*] He threw this in the fireplace, and it didn't burn.

MONTAGUE. Bullen!

JACK. In Grimes' own handwriting: "My Dear Porter—I will call" . . . you can see what that word was . . "at eight-thirty. Very urgent." How's that?

MONTAGUE. Man, it's ghastly! [*A pause.*] How did you manage to get these?

JACK. It's a long story.

MONTAGUE. How did Grimes work it? Money?

JACK. Not a dollar.

MONTAGUE. What then?

JACK. Just bluffed him. Party loyalty! What was he named for?

MONTAGUE. But in a suit like this!

JACK. Never was a better test! If Hegan lost this case, he'd be wiped off the slate, and the organization might go down at the next election. And what were you put in for, Judge Porter? Don't you see?

MONTAGUE. I see! It takes my breath away!

JACK. [*Looking about.*] And what a place for us to meet in! Did you see Grimes?

MONTAGUE. Yes.

JACK. I'll wager he came to tell Hegan about it.

MONTAGUE. No doubt of it.

JACK. God! I'd give one hand to have heard them!

MONTAGUE. Don't wish that! It's embarrassing enough as it is!

JACK. [*Staring at him.*] You'll see it through? You won't back out?

MONTAGUE. Oh, I'll see it through . . . trust me for that. But it's devilish awkward!

JACK. Why did you come here?

MONTAGUE. I tried not to. But Miss Hegan insisted.

JACK. [*Laughing.*] The same here! I was fair caught!

MONTAGUE. And now she'll think we learned it here. I'll have to explain to her . . .

JACK. What?

MONTAGUE. I must!

JACK. No! [LAURA *appears at windows, centre, and hears the rest, which is in excited tones.*] It is not to be thought of!

MONTAGUE. But I can't help it, man! Miss Hegan will think I've been eavesdropping!

JACK. Do you realize what you're proposing, man? You'll ruin everything! We've got Grimes dead . . . we can land him in jail! But if Hegan heard any whisper of it, they'd balk everything!

MONTAGUE. But how?

JACK. They'd hold up the decision of the Court . . .

MONTAGUE. Nonsense! With all that they'd stand to lose . . .

LAURA. [*Coming forward.*] I beg pardon, Mr. Bullen.

JACK. Oh!

LAURA. I didn't wish to hear what you were saying. But I couldn't help it. I was caught unawares. [*The three stare at each other.*] It is something that involves my father. [*Looking at the papers in* BULLEN'S *hands.*] Mr. Bullen has brought you some evidence. Is that so, Mr. Montague?

MONTAGUE. [*In a low voice.*] Yes, Miss Hegan.

LAURA. And you wished to take me into your confidence?

MONTAGUE. I wished to make it impossible for you to think we had obtained this evidence in your home.

LAURA. I see.

MONTAGUE. You will do us the justice to recognize that we did not seek admission here.

LAURA. Yes; I do that. [*A pause.*] All that I can say is, that if you think it best to take me into your confidence, you may trust me to the bitter end.

MONTAGUE. Miss Hegan, Mr. Bullen has brought me evidence which proves that the decision of the Court, which is to be made known to-morrow, has been . . . improperly affected.

LAURA. [*Quickly.*] By whom?

MONTAGUE. By Robert Grimes.

LAURA. [*Starts wildly.*] And the evidence involves my father?

MONTAGUE. Your father will be the chief one to profit from the change.

LAURA. [*Sinks back against the table; stares away from them, whispering.*] To Grimes . . . two hundred thousand on Court deal! I see! I see! [*Faces them, weakly.*] And what . . . what do you mean to do?

MONTAGUE. I intend to wait until the decision has been announced, which will be to-morrow, and then to call a public meeting and present the evidence.

LAURA. [*Starts to implore him; then controls herself.*] Yes, yes . . . that is just. But then . . . see! It hasn't been done yet!

MONTAGUE. How do you mean?

LAURA. The decision hasn't come out. It could be stopped!

JACK. Why stop it?

LAURA. That would prevent the wrong! I would . . . oh, I see! You want to expose Grimes! You'd rather it happened!

JACK. The crime has already been committed.

LAURA. And you, Mr. Montague . . . you prefer it so?

MONTAGUE. I had never thought of any other possibility.

LAURA. Listen! I don't understand the matter very clearly. The Grand Avenue Railroad case . . .

MONTAGUE. It is an effort to annul a franchise which was obtained by proven bribery.

LAURA. Then, if the public could win, it would be worth while, would it not?

MONTAGUE. It would establish a precedent of vast importance. But how could that be done?

LAURA. We have a hold upon these men . . . we could compel them to give way!

MONTAGUE. They would never do it, Miss Hegan . . . they have too much at stake.

LAURA. But . . . the evidence you have! Mr. Bullen said you could send Grimes to jail.

MONTAGUE. That was just wild talk. Grimes has the district attorney and the courts. He could never be punished for anything.

LAURA. But the exposure!

JACK. He's been exposed a hundred times. What does that matter to him?

LAURA. But then . . . my father is involved.

JACK. Quite true, Miss Hegan . . .

LAURA. And I can make him see how wrong it is.

JACK. You can make him see it! But you can't make him do anything!

LAURA. Ah, but you don't know my father . . . truly, you don't. He does these evil things, but at heart he's a kind and loyal man! And he loves me . . . I am his only daughter . . . and I can help him to see what is right. We have always understood each other; he will listen to me as he would not to any one else in the world.

JACK. But what can you say to him? We can't put our evidence in your hands . . .

LAURA. I don't need your evidence. I must tell you that I, too, have found out something about this case. I know that my father paid Mr. Grimes to influence the decision of that Court. And I know how much he paid him.

MONTAGUE. Miss Hegan!

JACK. Good God!

LAURA. You see, I am not afraid to trust you. . . . [*A pause.*] What is the nature of your evidence against Grimes?

MONTAGUE. It comes from an eye-witness of his interview with the Judge.

LAURA. And it is some one you can trust?

MONTAGUE. It's for Bullen to tell you.

JACK. The Judge has a nephew, a dissipated chap, whose inheritance he is holding back . . . and who hates him in consequence. The nephew happens to be a college chum of mine. He witnessed the interview and he brought me the evidence.

LAURA. I see. Then, certainly, I have a case. And don't you see what a hold that gives me upon my father?

JACK. Miss Hegan, you are a brave woman, and I would like to give way to you. But you could accomplish nothing. This suit, which is nominally in the public interest, is really backed by Murdock and his crowd, who are fighting your father; you must realize his position . . . the thousand ties that bind him . . . all the habits of a lifetime! Think of the friends he has to protect; you don't know . . .

LAURA. I know it all. And, on the other hand, I know some things that you do not know. I know that my father is not a happy man. There is a canker eating at his heart . . . the fruit of life has turned to ashes on his lips. And he has one person in all this world that he loves . . . myself. He has toiled and fought for me . . . all these years he has told himself that he was making his money for me. And now he finds that it brings me only misery and grief . . . it is as useless to me as it is to him! And now, suppose I should go to him and say: "Father, you have committed a crime. And I cannot stand it another hour. You must choose here and now . . . you must give up this fight against the people . . . you must give up this career, and come with me and help me to do good in the world. Or else" . . . [*her voice breaking.*] . . . "I shall have to leave you! I shall refuse to touch a dollar of your money; I shall refuse in any way to share your guilt!" Don't you see? He will know that I am speaking the truth . . . and that I mean every word of it. Oh, gentlemen, believe me . . . my father would be as strong to atone for his injustices as he has been to commit them! Surely, you can't refuse me this chance to save him?

JACK. Miss Hegan . . .

MONTAGUE. For God's sake, Jack . . .

JACK. Excuse me, Montague. How long would you expect us to wait, Miss Hegan?

LAURA. You need not wait at all. You could go right ahead with your own plans. Meantime, I can go to my father . . . I will have to-night to plead with him, and to-morrow morning you will know if I have succeeded.

JACK. Very well . . . I will consent to that.

LAURA. Let Mr. Montague come to my father's office to-morrow morning at ten o'clock. I shall not give him up . . . even if I have to follow him there! And now . . . good-bye . . . [*Starts toward the door, breaks down and cries.*] Thank you! Thank you!
Stretches out her hands to them.

MONTAGUE. [*Springing toward her.*] Miss Hegan!

LAURA. Give me a little courage! Tell me you think I shall succeed!

MONTAGUE. [*Seizing her hand.*] I believe you will, Miss Hegan!

LAURA. Ah! Thank you!

MONTAGUE. [*Kisses her hand; tries to speak; overcome.*] Good-bye!

LAURA. [*Exit.*] Ah, God!

JACK. I understand, old man! If only she weren't so rich!

MONTAGUE. If only she weren't . . .

JACK. Yes, yes, dear boy; I know how it is. You're troubled with a conscience, and yours must be strictly a cottage affair! But forget it just now, old fellow . . . we've got work before us. Play ball!

Takes him by the shoulder; they go off.

CURTAIN

ACT III

HEGAN'S *office in Wall street. A large room, furnished with severe simplicity. At the left a large table, with half a dozen chairs about it, and a "ticker" near the wall; at the right, a flat-topped desk and a telephone. Entrance centre.*

At rise: ANDREWS *stands by desk; takes some papers, looks them over, makes note and replaces them.*

PARKER. [*Enters.*] Say, Andrews, what's the reply to these letters of the Fourth National?

ANDREWS. Give them here; I'll see to them.

PARKER. Any orders for the brokers this morning?

ANDREWS. I'm writing them myself.

PARKER. Something special, eh? All right. [*Looks at ticker.*] Hello! Listen to this: "There is a rumor, widely current, that the decision of the Court of Appeals in the matter of the Public *vs.* the Grand Avenue Railroad Company will be handed down to-day!" Gee whiz, I wonder if that's so?

ANDREWS. I have heard the rumor.

PARKER. There was a reporter here yesterday, trying to pump me. I'll bet they're watching the boss.

ANDREWS. Yes; no doubt of that.

PARKER. Cracky! I'd like to know which way it'll go!

ANDREWS. A good many others would like to know, I've no doubt.

PARKER. I'll bet my hat the boss knows!

ANDREWS. It may be.

A pause; PARKER *continues to read ticker.*

ACT III] THE MACHINE 119

PARKER. I don't suppose you've heard anything, have you?

ANDREWS. I never hear, Parker.

PARKER. Oh, say . . . come off. Why don't you drop a fellow a hint now and then?

ANDREWS. I can't afford to.

PARKER. It would never go beyond me. [*A pause.*] Say, Andrews.

ANDREWS. Well?

PARKER. Would you like to invest a bit for me now and then?

ANDREWS. I'm not hankering to, especially.

PARKER. I'll go halves with you on the profits.

ANDREWS. And how about the losses?

PARKER. There wouldn't be any losses.

ANDREWS. Cut it out, Parker . . . we don't want that kind of a thing in the office. [*Handing him paper.*] Here . . . I want three copies of this. And take my advice and live on your salary.

PARKER. Thanks. I wish the salary increased as fast as the bills do! [*Starts to door; sees* LAURA.] Oh! Good morning, Miss Hegan!

LAURA. [*Enters hurriedly.*] Good morning.

ANDREWS. Good morning, Miss Hegan.

PARKER *exit*.

LAURA. Mr. Andrews, where was my father last night?

ANDREWS. He had an important conference . . .

LAURA. He did not come to the house.

ANDREWS. No, Miss Hegan; it was too late. He stayed downtown . . .

LAURA. And you were not home, either.

ANDREWS. I was with him.

LAURA. It is too bad! I have been trying all night to find either of you.

ANDREWS. Why . . . your father had no idea when he left . . .

LAURA. I know. Something has turned up . . .

ANDREWS. Nothing wrong, I hope.

LAURA. I must see my father as soon as possible. He will be here this morning?

ANDREWS. Any minute, Miss Hegan.

LAURA. He will surely come?

ANDREWS. Not the slightest doubt of it. Nothing could keep him away.

LAURA. I wish to see him the moment he comes. And if he should call up or send word . . .

ANDREWS. I will see that he is informed, Miss Hegan.

LAURA. Thank you. [*A pause.*] The Court decision is expected to-day, is it not, Mr. Andrews?

ANDREWS. [*Hesitates.*] There has been a rumor, Miss Hegan.

LAURA. And so there will be considerable disturbance of the market?

ANDREWS. Presumably.

LAURA. And my father has made preparations?

ANDREWS. Yes.

LAURA. That is what the conference was about?

ANDREWS. I presume so, Miss Hegan.

LAURA. By the way, Mr. Andrews, I expect Mr. Montague here at ten o'clock. Please let me know when he comes.

ANDREWS. Yes, Miss Hegan. [*Goes to the door, then turns.*] Here is Mr. Hegan now.

LAURA. [*Starting up.*] Ah!

ANDREWS. [*Holding open door.*] Good morning, Mr. Hegan.

HEGAN. [*Enters.*] Good morning.

LAURA. Father!

HEGAN. Why, Laura! [ANDREWS *exit*.] What are you doing here?

LAURA. I've come to have a talk with you.

HEGAN. To have a talk with me?

LAURA. Come in, please, father. Shut the door.

HEGAN. Yes, my dear; but . . .

LAURA. I came into the city on the next train after you. I have been hunting for you ever since . . . I have been up all night. I have something of the utmost urgency to talk with you about.

HEGAN. What is it?

LAURA. Come and sit down, please.

HEGAN. Yes, my dear.

LAURA. Listen, father. Yesterday afternoon, when we were talking, you told me that you had never done anything to influence the courts in their decisions.

HEGAN. Yes, Laura.

LAURA. And you told me that nobody else ever did it, either for you or for your companies.

HEGAN. Yes, but . . .

LAURA. And, father, you told me a falsehood.

HEGAN. Laura!

LAURA. I am very sorry, but I have to say it. It was a falsehood; and it is but one of many falsehoods that you have told me. I understand just why you did it . . . you think I ought not to ask about these things, because it will make me unhappy; and so, for my own good, you do not hesitate to tell me things that are not true.

HEGAN. My child, it is your father that you are talking to!

LAURA. It is my father, and a father who knows that I love him very dearly, and who will realize it hurts me to say these things, fully as much as it hurts him to hear them. But they must be said . . . and said now.

HEGAN. Why now? Just at this moment . . .

LAURA. I know what you are going to say. At this moment you are very busy . . .

HEGAN. My dear, the Exchange will open in an hour. And I am in the midst of a big campaign. I have important orders for my brokers, and a hundred other matters to attend to. And I expect Grimes here any minute . . .

LAURA. Grimes?

HEGAN. Yes, my dear.

LAURA. You are not through with him yet, then?

HEGAN. No, Laura . . .

LAURA. Well, even so! Mr. Grimes must wait until I have said what I have to say to you.

HEGAN. What is it, Laura?

LAURA. You are expecting the decision of the Court of Appeals on the Grand Avenue Railroad case at noon to-day.

HEGAN. Why, yes . . .

LAURA. The decision will be in your favor. And you and Grimes are planning to gamble on it, and to make a great deal of money.

HEGAN. Yes, my dear.

LAURA. And you paid Grimes two hundred thousand dollars to fix the decision of the Court.

HEGAN. [*Starting violently.*] Laura!

LAURA. Grimes went to Judge Porter's house the night before last and induced him to change his vote on the case.

HEGAN. Laura!

LAURA And so, what was to have been the minority opinion of the Court is to be given out to-day as the Court's decision.

HEGAN. My God!

LAURA. You do not deny that this is the truth?

HEGAN. You overheard us at the house!

LAURA. Not one word, father.

HEGAN. But you must have!

LAURA. Father, throughout this conversation, you may honor me by assuming that I am telling you the absolute truth. And I will be glad when you will give me the same privilege.

HEGAN. Then, how did you learn it?

LAURA. That, unfortunately, I am not at liberty to tell you.

HEGAN. Then other people know it?

LAURA. They do.

HEGAN. Good God! [*Stares at her, dumbfounded.*] Who are these people?

LAURA. I cannot tell you that.

HEGAN. But, Laura . . . you must!

LAURA. It is impossible.

HEGAN. But . . . how can that be?

LAURA. I cannot discuss the matter.

HEGAN. But think . . . my dear! I am your father, and you must trust me . . . you must help me . . .

LAURA. Please do not ask me. I have given my word.

HEGAN. Your word! [*Gazes about, distracted.*] You take the part of others against your own flesh and blood!

LAURA. Listen, father! Think of me for a minute, and how it seems to me. Do not be so ignoble as to think only of the exposure . . .

HEGAN. But, my child, realize what it will mean if this comes out! Are these people among my enemies?

LAURA. That depends upon circumstances.

HEGAN. I don't understand you.

LAURA. I will try to explain, if you will be patient with me.

HEGAN. Go on! Go on!

LAURA. Father, you know what has been happening to me during the past few months. You know how unhappy

I have been. And now you have committed a crime . . . a dreadful, dreadful crime!

HEGAN. My dear!

LAURA. I wish to make it clear to you . . . I am in desperate earnest. I have taken all night to think it over, and I am not making any mistake. I have made up my mind that, come what will, and cost what it may, I must clear myself of the responsibility for these evils.

HEGAN. In what way are you responsible?

LAURA. In every way imaginable. My whole life is based upon them . . . everything that I have and enjoy is stained with the guilt of them . . . the house in which I live, the clothing that I wear, the food that I eat. And I shall never again know what it is to be happy, while I have that fact upon my conscience. Don't you see?

HEGAN. I see.

LAURA. I tried all night to find you. I wanted to have a chance to talk with you, quietly. And, now, instead, I have to do it here, amid all the rush and strain of this dreadful Wall Street. But so it is . . . I must say it here. Father, I have come to plead with you, to plead with you upon my knees. Listen to me . . . don't turn me away!

HEGAN. What do you wish me to do?

LAURA. First of all, I wish you to give up this illegal advantage that you have gained. I wish you to stop this decision, and give the people the victory to which they are entitled.

HEGAN. But, my dear, that is madness! How can I . . .

LAURA. You compelled Grimes to do this thing . . . you can compel him to undo it!

HEGAN. But, my dear, it would ruin me!

LAURA. If you do what I ask you to do, ruin will not matter.

HEGAN. What do you ask me?

LAURA. I wish you to stop this mad career . . . to give up this money game . . . to drop it utterly! To stop selling stocks and manipulating markets; to stop buying politicians and franchises . . . to sell out everything . . . to withdraw. I want you to do it now . . . to-day . . . this very hour!

HEGAN. But, my dear . . .

LAURA. I want you to come with me, and help me to find happiness again, by doing some good in the world. I want you to use your power and your talents to help people, instead of to destroy them.

HEGAN. My child! That is something very easy to talk about, but not so easy to do!

LAURA. We will work together, and find ways to do it.

HEGAN. It seems possible, from your point of view . . . with your noble ideals, and your sheltered life . . .

LAURA. My sheltered life! That is just what I can no longer endure! That I should have ease and comfort, while others suffer . . . that my father should take part in this mad struggle for money and power, in order to give me a sheltered life! I must make it impossible for that to continue! I must make you understand that all your money is powerless to bring me happiness . . . that it is poisoning my life as well as your own!

HEGAN. [*Gravely.*] Laura, I have tried to protect you . . . that is the natural instinct of a father . . . to keep evil things from his daughter's knowledge. If I have told you untruths, as you say, that has been the one reason. But since you will not have it so . . . since you must face the facts of the world . . .

LAURA. I must!

HEGAN. Very well, then . . . you shall face them. You tell me to give up this case . . . to change back the Court's decision, so that the public may reap the advantage. Do you realize that the public has nothing to do with this suit? . . . That it is a covert attack upon me by an unscrupulous enemy?

LAURA. You mean Murdock?

HEGAN. Murdock. You know something of his career, perhaps . . . something of his private life, too. And if I should turn back, as you ask, the public would gain nothing . . . he would be the only one to profit. He would raid my securities; he would throw my companies into bankruptcy; he would draw my associates away from me . . . in the end, he would take my place in the traction field. Is that what you wish to bring about?

LAURA. It is not that that I am thinking of. It is the corrupting of the Court . . .

HEGAN. The Court! Do you know why Grimes and I had to do what we did?

LAURA. No.

HEGAN. And yet you have judged me! What would you say if I told you that we had information that one of the judges had received a thousand shares of Grand Avenue stock from Murdock? And that another had been promised a seat in the United States Supreme Court by that eminent Republican?

LAURA. Oh! Horrible!

HEGAN. You see what the game is?

LAURA. But, father! The buying and selling of the powers of the Government . . .

HEGAN. The "Government" consisting of politicians who have gotten themselves elected for the purpose of selling out to the highest bidder. For ten years now I have been in charge of these properties . . . I have had the interests of thousands of investors in my keeping . . . and all the while I have been like a man surrounded by a pack of wolves. I defended myself as I could . . . in the end, I found that the best way to defend was by attacking. In other words, I had to go into politics, to make the control of the "Government" a part of my business. Don't you see?

LAURA. Yes, I see. But why play such a game?

HEGAN. Why? Because it is the only game I have ever known . . . the only game there is to play. That is the way I have lived my life . . . the way I have risen to power and command. I played it for myself, and for my friends, and for those I loved.

LAURA. You played it for me! And, oh! father! father! . . . Can't you see what that means to me? To realize that all my life has been based upon such things! Don't you see how I can't let it go on . . . how, if you refuse to do what I ask you to, it will be impossible for me to touch a dollar of your money?

HEGAN. Laura!

LAURA. Just that, father! I should never again be able to face my conscience!

HEGAN. [*After a pause.*] Listen to me, dear. You know that I have always meant to withdraw . . .

LAURA. I know that. And that has been a confession! You know that you are wrecking your life—wrecking everything! And if you mean to stop, why not stop?

HEGAN. But, my dear, at this moment . . . in the midst of the battle . . .

LAURA. At this moment you are on the point of doing something that will put a brand upon your conscience for the balance of your career. And at this moment you are confronted with the realization that you are ruining your daughter's life. You see her before you, desperate . . . frantic with shame and grief. And you have to make up your mind, either to drive her from you, heartbroken . . . or else to turn your face from these evils, and to take up a new way of life.

HEGAN. [*Broken and crushed, sits staring at her.*] Laura!

LAURA. [*Stretching out her arms to him.*] Father!
A knock at the door; they start.

GRIMES. [*Enters.*] Oh! Beg pardon!

HEGAN. Come in.

LAURA. [*Starting up.*] No!

HEGAN. Come in! You must know it!

GRIMES. What is it?

HEGAN. Shut the door! Grimes, the game is up!

GRIMES. How d'ye mean?

HEGAN. We've been betrayed. Somebody knows all about the Court decision . . . about what passed between you and Porter, and between you and me!

GRIMES. The hell you say!

HEGAN. We're threatened with exposure!

GRIMES. Who is it?

HEGAN. I don't know.

GRIMES. But, then . . .

HEGAN. My daughter tells me. But she is not at liberty to give the names.

GRIMES. Well, I'll be damned! [*He stares from* HEGAN *to* LAURA; *then comes and sits, very deliberately, where he can gaze at them. A long pause; then, nodding toward* LAURA.] What's her game?

HEGAN. [*Weakly.*] She will tell you.

GRIMES. [*Looking at her.*] Well?

LAURA. I am here to plead with my father to turn back from this wickedness.

GRIMES. [*Stares.*] And do what, ma'am?

LAURA. Quit Wall Street, and devote himself to some useful work.

GRIMES. [*After a pause.*] And if he won't?

LAURA. I have told him he must choose between his present career and his daughter's love.

GRIMES. [*Gazes at* LAURA, *then in front of him; slowly shakes his head.*] I can't make out our young people.

When I was a boy, young women looked up to their parents. What's your father done to you, that you should turn against him?

LAURA. I have not turned against him, Mr. Grimes.

GRIMES. [*Indicating* HEGAN, *who sits in an attitude of despair.*] Look at him!

A pause.

LAURA. I am pleading with him for his own good . . . to give up this cruel struggle . . .

GRIMES. To turn tail and run from his enemies?

LAURA. It is of my duty to the public that I am thinking, Mr. Grimes.

GRIMES. You owe no duty to this world higher than your duty to your father.

LAURA. You think that?

GRIMES. I think it.

LAURA. [*Hesitates a moment, then turns.*] Father! What do you say? Is that true?

HEGAN. [*Crushed.*] I don't know, my dear.

GRIMES. God Almighty! And this is Jim Hegan! [*To* LAURA.] Where'd you get onto these ideas, ma'am?

LAURA. [*In a low voice.*] I think, Mr. Grimes, it might be best if you did not ask me to discuss this question. Our points of view are too different.

GRIMES. [*Shrugs his shoulders.*] As you please, ma'am. But you needn't mind me . . . I ain't easy to offend. And I'm only trying to understand you.

LAURA. [*After a silence.*] Mr. Grimes, I had the good fortune to be brought up in a beautiful and luxurious home; but not long ago I began to go down into the slums and see the homes of the people. I saw sights that made me sick with horror.

GRIMES. No doubt, ma'am.

LAURA. I found the people in the grip of a predatory

organization that had bound them hand and foot, and was devouring them alive.

GRIMES. You've been listening to tales, ma'am. We do a lot for the people.

LAURA. You treat them to free coal and free picnics and free beer, and so you get their votes; and then you sell them out to capitalists like my father.

GRIMES. Humph!

LAURA. You sell them out to any one, high or low, who will pay for the privilege of exploiting them. You sell them to the rum-dealer and the dive-keeper and the gambler. You sell them to the white-slave trader.

GRIMES. There's no such person, Miss Hegan.

LAURA. You offer an insult to my intelligence, Mr. Grimes. I have met with him and his work. There was a girl of the slums . . . her name was Annie Rogers. She was a decent girl; and she was lured into a dive and drugged and shut up in a brothel, a prisoner. She escaped to the street, pursued, and a friend of mine saved her. And, high and low, among the authorities of this city, we sought for justice for that girl, and there was no justice to be had. Yesterday afternoon I learned that she cut her own throat.

GRIMES. I see.

LAURA. And that happened, Mr. Grimes! It happened in the City of New York! I saw it with my own eyes!

GRIMES. Such things have been, ma'am.

LAURA. And you permit them.

GRIMES. I?

LAURA. You permit them!

GRIMES. I can't attempt to discuss prostitution with a lady. Such things existed long before I was born.

LAURA. You could use your power to drive the traffic from the city.

GRIMES. Yes, ma'am; I suppose I could. But if I'd

been that sort of a man, do you think I'd ever had the power?

LAURA. How neatly parried! What sort of a man are you, anyway?

GRIMES. [*Looks at her fixedly.*] I'll tell you the sort of man I am, ma'am. [*A pause.*] I wasn't brought up in a beautiful, luxurious home. I was brought up with five brothers, in two rooms on the top floor of a rear tenement on Avenue B; I was a little street "mick," and then I was a prize "scrapper," and the leader of a gang. When a policeman chased me upstairs, my mother stood at the head and fought him off with a rolling-pin. That was the way we stood by our children, ma'am; and we looked to them to stand by us. Once, when I was older, my enemies tried to do me . . . they charged me with a murder that I never done, ma'am. But d'ye think my old father ever stopped to ask if I done it or not, ma'am? Not much. "Don't mention that, Bob, my boy," says he . . . "it's all part of the fight, an' we're wid yer." [*A pause.*] I looked about me at the world, ma'am, and I found it was full of all sorts of pleasant things, that I'd never had, and never stood a chance of havin'. They were for the rich . . . the people on top. And they looked on with scorn . . . I was poor and I was low, and I wasn't fit for anything And so I set to climb, ma'am. I shouldered my way up. I met men that fought me; I fought them back, and I won out. That's the sort of man I am.

LAURA. I see. A selfish man, bent upon power at any price! A brutal man, profiting by the weakness of others! An unscrupulous man, trading upon fear and greed! A man who has stopped at no evil to gain his purpose!

GRIMES. I am what the game has made me.

LAURA. Not so! Not so! Many another man has been born to a fate like yours, and has fought his way up from the pit . . . to be a tower of strength for goodness and service, an honor to his people and himself.

GRIMES. I've not met any such, ma'am.

LAURA. No; you've not sought for them. You did not need them in your business. The men you needed were the thugs and the criminals, who could stuff ballot-boxes for you . . . the dive-keepers and the vice-sellers, who would contribute to your campaign funds! And you have dealt with them . . . you have built up the power they gave you into a mighty engine of corruption and wrong! And you are master of it . . . you use it to wring tribute from high and low! Selling immunity to dive-keepers and betraying helpless young girls! Naming legislators and judges, and receiving bribes to corrupt the highest Court in the State.

HEGAN. Laura . . .

LAURA. Father, I did not seek this discussion! He challenged me . . . and he shall hear the truth! For all these months the thing that has been driving me to desperation has been the knowledge that my father was the business associate and ally of a master of infamy like Robert Grimes!

GRIMES. Thanks, ma'am! And so now he's to break with me!

A knock at the door.

ANDREWS. [*Enters, centre.*] Mr. Hegan, these orders for your brokers must be signed.

HEGAN. I won't sign them!

ANDREWS. Sir?

HEGAN. Never mind them.

GRIMES. [*Springing to his feet.*] Jim Hegan, you're mad! [*To* ANDREWS.] Go out, will you? [ANDREWS *exit.*] Hegan, man . . . surely you don't mean this?

HEGAN. Yes . . . I'm sick of it!

GRIMES. But, man, think of the rest of us! . . . What are we to do?

HEGAN. You can buy just the same.

GRIMES. But without you? Why, we won't be able to corner Murdock! And if he gets out of this hole, it'll be worse than ever! There'll be hell to pay!

HEGAN. I don't care.

GRIMES. But, man, you've pledged yourself! Look at what Harris has done! . . . What excuse will you be able to make to him? And what will you tell Henry Stevens?

HEGAN. I'll tell them I've quit.

GRIMES. But you told them last night you were going in with every dollar you could raise! You told Isaacson he could break with Murdock! And now you'll tell them you've turned tail and run! Why, Hegan, it's treason!

HEGAN. Listen to me . . .

GRIMES. I don't want to listen to you! Half an hour from now you'll be ashamed of yourself . . . wishing that nobody had heard you! You'll be begging me not to mention it! You . . . Jim Hegan . . . the traction king! To lose your nerve over a little thing like this! What's come over you, anyhow . . . after all the things we've been through together? Why, man . . .

The 'phone rings.

HEGAN. Hello! Who is it? Oh, Isaacson. Yes; I'll speak with him. Hello, Isaacson! Yes. No; I've not forgotten. I'll do whatever I said I'd do. Er . . . yes; that's all right. I've been delayed. Yes. I'll get the money to you. Right away. Oh, certainly, that's all right. [*Hangs up receiver.*] Ah, God!

GRIMES. Hegan, listen here. You're in the midst of a battle. And you're the general. Everything depends on you this morning. And you've a right to be afraid . . . but you've no right to let others see it. You've no *right* . . . do you understand me? And, by God, I won't let you! . . . I'll be a man for two of you! Shake yourself together now! [*Seizes him.*] Come, man! Shake yourself together!

HEGAN. But think of the exposure!

GRIMES. The exposure! And this is Jim Hegan talking! How many times have you been exposed already? And how many times have I been?

HEGAN. But this is different.

GRIMES. How different? We've got the police, and we've got the district attorney, and we've got the courts. What more do we want? What can they do but talk in the newspapers? And is there anything they haven't said about us already? [*Takes* HEGAN *by the arm, and laughs.*] Come, old man! As my friend Leary says: "Dis is a nine-day town. If yez kin stand de gaff for nine days, ye're all right!" We'll stand the gaff!

HEGAN. I'm tired of standing it.

GRIMES. Yes, we all get tired now and then. But this afternoon it'll be Murdock that's tired. Think of him, Hegan . . . try to realize him a bit! You've got him where you want him at last! Remember what he did to you in the Brooklyn Ferry case! Remember how he lied to you in the Third Avenue case! And he told Isaacson, only last week, that he'd never let up on you till he'd driven you out of the traction field!

HEGAN. Did he say that?

GRIMES. He did that! And only yesterday he said he was getting ready to finish you! He's as sure of this Court decision as I am of the sunrise! I'm told he's short already over a quarter of a million shares!

HEGAN. But his judges'll get word to him . . . he'll buy!

GRIMES. Of course! But that's just why you ought to be busy! Buy first, and make him pay . . . damn his soul!

ANDREWS. [*Knocks and enters.*] Mr. Stevens is here, Mr. Hegan.

GRIMES. Henry Stevens? We'll see him. [ANDREWS *exit.*] Come on, man! We'll go over to your brokers and take the orders. It'll give you a smell of the powder smoke.

LAURA. [*As* HEGAN *starts to follow.*] Father, you are going with him?

HEGAN. My dear child, what can I do?

LAURA. But think of the disgrace . . . the shame of it! You will carry it with you all your life!

HEGAN. I can't help it. I am bound hand and foot. I . . .

LAURA. Father! [*She rushes to him, and flings her arms about him.*] Do you realize what you are doing? You are driving me away from you! . . . You are casting me off! And all for a few more dollars!

HEGAN. My dear, it is not that. My word is pledged.

LAURA. You are trampling me in the dust. You are spurning all that is best in your life!

GRIMES. Come, come, man! The game is called!

HEGAN. Let me go, my dear.

LAURA. Father!

HEGAN. No! No! [*He gently, but firmly, puts her arms from him.*] Good-bye, dear.

LAURA. Father! [HEGAN *and* GRIMES *go out centre; she sinks by the table, and buries her face in her arms, sobbing; after a considerable interval, a knock on the door, centre.*] Come in!

MONTAGUE. [*Enters.*] Well?

LAURA. I have failed. [*Rises and stretches out her arms.*] Failed! He has gone with Grimes!

MONTAGUE. I saw him go, Miss Hegan.

LAURA. [*Swiftly.*] And yet . . . I have not failed

utterly. I have failed to turn back the decision . . . to save him from this disgrace. But that is not all.

MONTAGUE. How do you mean?

LAURA. I shall not give him up . . . and, in the end, I shall have my way; I can see that quite clearly. Ah, how I hurt him! I almost broke his heart! And just now he is in the midst of the battle . . . the rage of it is on him. But, afterwards, he will recollect . . . he will be overwhelmed with grief! And then he will see! He will do what I have begged him to!

MONTAGUE. Yes . . . perhaps that is so.

LAURA. I know what my love means to him! I know what he is at heart! And when he sees that I mean to carry out my threat, to go by myself and to refuse to touch his money . . . that will be more than he can bear, Mr. Montague!

MONTAGUE. You mean to do that?

LAURA. I mean to do it! I mean to do it to-day; and I will never yield to him . . . never until he has atoned for this wrong he has done! And don't you see that I will win in the end?

MONTAGUE. Yes; I see.

LAURA. [*Quickly.*] Understand, that has nothing to do with your course. I am not asking you to spare him. You must go ahead and do your duty . . . you must do just what you would have done if I had never stood in the way.

MONTAGUE. It is a terrible thing to me, Miss Hegan. I cannot turn back . . .

LAURA. You must not! You must not think of it! It will be a part of my father's punishment . . . and he has deserved it. He has prepared that cup, and he must drink it . . . to the dregs!

MONTAGUE. You can bear it?

LAURA. It is not any question of what I can bear. It

is a question of the rights of the people. I saw that quite clearly, as my father talked with me. Whether it is he who wins, or whether it is Murdock, it is always the people that lose. And, let it hurt whom it may, the people must have the truth!

MONTAGUE. And then . . . you will be able to forgive me! Ah, what a weight you lift from me! I hardly dared to face the thought of what I had to do! [*Hesitating.*] And then, the thought that you mean to renounce your father's wealth . . . that you are going out into the world . . . alone . . .

LAURA. It will not be hard for me. You cannot know how I have hated my past life. To know that my father has plundered the public . . . and then to give his money, and call it charity. To be flattered and fawned upon . . . to be celebrated and admired . . . and never for anything that I am, but always for my money!

MONTAGUE. I understand what you feel! And see what your decision means to me . . . it sets me free at last!

LAURA. Free!

MONTAGUE. Free to speak! Miss Hegan, I came to New York, and I met these rich people, and I saw how their fortunes were poisoning their lives. I saw men who could not have a real friend in the world, because of their money. I saw young girls whose souls were utterly dead in them because they had been brought up to think of themselves as keepers of money-bags, and to guard against men who sought to prey upon them. I hated the thing . . . I fled from it as I would from a plague. In that world I had met a woman I might have loved . . . a woman who was noble and beautiful and true; and yet I dared not speak to her . . I dared not even permit myself to know her . . . because I was a poor man, and she was rich. But now she is to be poor also! And so I may speak!

THE SECOND-STORY MAN

CHARACTERS

JIM FARADAY: the second-story man.
HARVEY AUSTIN: a lawyer.
HELEN AUSTIN: his wife.

SCENE: Library of the Austin home.
TIME: 2 A. M.

THE SECOND-STORY MAN

The scene shows a luxuriously furnished room. In the centre is a table with a lamp. To the right is the entrance into the front hall, the front door of the house being visible. In the corner is a cabinet of curios. In the rear is a large window opening on the street. Open fire-place. There are two entrances at the left. There are book-shelves, several easy-chairs, etc., in the room.

At rise: The stage is empty, and the room is darkened except for the fire in the grate. Sounds of breaking wood are heard at the window.

JIM. [*A roughly-dressed young fellow with a patch over one eye, enters through window, stands gazing about nervously, looks into the hall, etc., then flashes a dark lantern.*] This looks pretty good.

Goes to mantel, takes silver cup and puts it into bag which he carries; then exit left.

AUSTIN. [*Enters at front door without much noise. Hangs up coat and hat, and then stands in entrance. He is a smooth-faced young man in evening dress.*] All gone to bed, hey?

Takes out cigarette case and is about to light one, when a crash is heard off left, as of a vase falling. He starts, then runs to table, opens drawer, takes out revolver, and examines it, and steals off through the other entrance at left, saying, "*That noise seemed to come from downstairs.*"

JIM. [*Enters panic-stricken.*] God! What a thing to do! [*Gazes into hall and upstairs—long pause.*] Don't seem to have waked them.

Proceeds to examine room, stopping now and then to listen. After placing several articles in bag, he goes to cabinet and tries to open it. This takes some time, and while he is crouching in the shadow, with his back to the entrance right, MRS. AUSTIN *appears.*

MRS. AUSTIN. [*She is young and beautiful, and wears a night-robe and dressing-gown. She stands looking about anxiously, and then goes to centre of room, when she hears a sound from* JIM, *and starts wildly.*] Oh!

JIM. [*Leaps to feet, lifting revolver.*] Hold up your hands! [*She starts back in terror.*] Hold up your hands!

MRS. AUSTIN. [*Half complyingly.*] I'm not armed.

JIM. Never mind. [*Long pause while they stare at each other.*] I don't want to hurt you, lady.

MRS. AUSTIN. [*Calmly, after first shock.*] No, I suppose not. You only want to get away.

JIM. That's right!

MRS. AUSTIN. Very well, you may go.

JIM. And you yell for the police the moment I get out of the door, hey?

MRS. AUSTIN. No, I don't want the police. I don't believe in sending men to jail.

JIM. Humph!

Another pause.

MRS. AUSTIN. Why do you do this?

JIM. It's the way I live.

MRS. AUSTIN. Isn't it a rather trying kind of work?

JIM. It ain't all play, ma'am.

MRS. AUSTIN. [*Smiling.*] I should think it would be

hard on the nerves. [*After another pause.*] Is there no honest way you can earn a living?

JIM. I don't know. Maybe so. I got tired of looking for it.

MRS. AUSTIN. I might help you if you would let me.

JIM. I ain't asking any help.

MRS. AUSTIN. No, but I'm offering it. [*After a pause.*] Have you been doing this sort of thing very long?

JIM. No.

MRS. AUSTIN. How long?

JIM. [*After hesitation.*] This is my first job.

MRS. AUSTIN. What! You don't mean that?

JIM. It happens to be true, ma'am.

MRS. AUSTIN. What made you do it?

JIM. It's a long story.

MRS. AUSTIN. Tell it to me.

JIM. It ain't just a good time for story telling.

MRS. AUSTIN. You are afraid of me? I have no quarrel with you. I don't care anything for the things you have in the bag; and, besides, I suppose you won't take them now. I'm only sorry to see a man going wrong, and I'd like to help if I could. I'll play fair, I give you my word of honor.

JIM. There ain't much honor in this business.

MRS. AUSTIN. No, I suppose not. But you can trust me. Put up that gun and talk to me.

JIM. [*Surlily.*] It can't do any good.

MRS. AUSTIN. It can't do any harm. Put up that revolver, and tell me what's the matter.

JIM. You'll let me go when I want to? No tricks!

MRS. AUSTIN. I give you my word.

JIM. All right. I'm a fool, I guess, but I'll trust you. [*Puts revolver in pocket.*] Sit down, ma'am. It must be cold for you. This is a queer kind of layout for a burglar.

[*Sits opposite her.*] You heard that racket I made in the other room?

MRS. AUSTIN. Yes. What was it?

JIM. Some kind of a jar.

MRS. AUSTIN. Oh, my Greek vase. Well, never mind . . . it was an imitation. What were you doing?

JIM. I was looking for something to eat.

MRS. AUSTIN. Oh!

JIM. It would have been the first thing I've had since the day before yesterday.

MRS. AUSTIN. What's the matter?

JIM. No work. [*A pause.*] I suppose you'll give me the old gag . . . there's plenty of work for a man that's willing.

MRS. AUSTIN. No, I happen to have studied, and I know better than that. Else I should have fainted when I saw you . . . instead of sitting here talking to you. . . . Do you drink?

JIM. Yes, but I didn't use to. Any man would drink . . . that went through what I did.

MRS. AUSTIN. Are you married?

JIM. Yes . . . I was married. My wife is dead.

MRS. AUSTIN. Any children?

JIM. Two. Both dead.

MRS. AUSTIN. Oh!

JIM. It ain't a pretty story, ma'am. It's a poor man's story.

MRS. AUSTIN. Tell it to me.

JIM. All right. It'll spoil your sleep for the rest of the night, I guess, but you can have it. [*A pause.*] A year ago I was what they call an honest working man. I had a home and a happy family; and I didn't drink any too much, and I did well . . . even if the work was hard. I was in the steel works here in town.

MRS. AUSTIN. [*Startled.*] The Empire Steel Company?

JIM. Yes. Why?

MRS. AUSTIN. Nothing . . . only I happen to know some people there. Go on.

JIM. It's no child's work there, ma'am. There's an awful lot of accidents . . . more than the world has any idea of. I've seen a man sent to hell in the snapping of a finger. And they don't treat them fair . . . they hush things up. There are things you wouldn't believe if I told them to you.

MRS. AUSTIN. Tell them.

JIM. I've seen a man there get caught in one of the cranes. They stopped the machinery, but they couldn't get him out. They'd have had to take the crane apart, and that would have cost several days, and it was rush time, and the man was only a poor Hunkie, and there was no one to know or care. So they started up the crane, and cut his leg off.

MRS. AUSTIN. Oh, horrible!

JIM. It's the sort of thing you couldn't believe unless you saw it. But I saw it. I didn't care, though. I was a fool. And then my time came.

MRS. AUSTIN. How do you mean?

JIM. A blast furnace blew out, and a piece of slag hit me here, where you see that patch. If it wasn't for the patch you'd see something that would make you sick. It was a pain you couldn't tell about . . . it was a couple of days before I knew where I was. And the first thing when I came to my senses . . . in the hospital, it was . . . there was a lawyer chap with a paper waiting for me.

MRS. AUSTIN. [*In agitation.*] A lawyer?

JIM. Yes, ma'am. Company representative, you know. And I was to sign the paper . . . it was a receipt for the hospital expenses . . . the operation and all that . . . you see they had to take out what was left of my eye.

And of course I couldn't see . . . I had to sign where he told me to. And when I got well, I found they had trapped me into signing a release.

MRS. AUSTIN. A release?

JIM. I had accepted the hospital expenses as a release for all the company owed me. And I couldn't get any damages . . . and my eye was gone, and all the weeks without any wages.

MRS. AUSTIN. My God!

JIM. And they turned me out so weak I could hardly walk; and . . .

MRS. AUSTIN. [*Greatly excited.*] Who was this man?

JIM. Which?

MRS. AUSTIN. This lawyer?

JIM. I never heard his name. He was a young fellow . . . handsome . . . smooth-faced . . .

MRS. AUSTIN. [*Whispering.*] Oh!

JIM. Ah, they don't mind it . . . they're smooth. They do that all the time. It's what they get their pay for.

MRS. AUSTIN. [*Covering her face with her hands.*] Oh, stop!

JIM. What's the matter?

MRS. AUSTIN. [*Looking up with white face.*] Nothing. Go on.

JIM. It was two months before I could work at all. And the rent came due, and they turned us out . . . it was winter-time, and my wife caught a cold, and it turned to pneumonia, and she died. That's all of that.

MRS. AUSTIN. Go on.

JIM. And then, you see, the panic came . . . and the mills shut down . . . sudden as that. The lawyer told me the company would see I always had a job, but that was only to get me to sign.

MRS. AUSTIN. [*Feverishly.*] Did you try him?

ACT I] **THE SECOND-STORY MAN** 147

JIM. I went to the office and tried; but they wouldn't even let me see him.

MRS. AUSTIN. I see. And then?

JIM. Then I went out to look for work. I had the two babies, you know . . . and God only knows how I loved those babies. I said I'd fight and win out for their sakes. But Amy . . . she was the little one . . . she never had been very strong. When you're a poor man, you can't get the best food, even if you know what it is. It ain't fit milk they sell for the children in this city; and the baby died . . . I never knew what was the matter exactly. And there was only one left . . . and me tramping the streets all day looking for a job. How was I to take care of him, lady? How could I have helped it? [*His voice is breaking with emotion.*] And oh, ma'am, he was the loveliest little fellow . . . with hair like gold. And so well and strong.

MRS. AUSTIN. [*Whispering.*] What happened to him?

JIM. A street car killed him.

MRS. AUSTIN. Oh!

JIM. Run over his chest, ma'am. I came home at night, and they told me, and I near went out of my mind. Can you think what it was to see him . . . with his eyes starting out of his head like, and his beautiful little body all mashed flat . . .

MRS. AUSTIN. [*Wildly.*] Oh, spare me!

JIM. I told you it wouldn't be a pretty story. Do you think maybe you wouldn't take to drink if you saw a sight like that? [*Sinking back.*] Since then I've looked for work, but I haven't cared much. Only sometimes I've thought I'd like to meet that young lawyer . . .

MRS. AUSTIN. [*Starting up.*] Oh!

JIM. Yes, it all began with him. But I don't know . . . they'd only jug me. Anyway, to-night I was sitting in a saloon with two fellows that I had met. One of them was a second-story man . . . a fellow that climbs up porches and fire-escapes. And I heard him telling about a haul he'd made, and I said to myself: "There's a job for me . . . I'll be a second-story man." And I tried it . . . but you see I didn't do very well. I'm not good for much, I guess, any more.

AUSTIN. [*Enters left, revolver in hand; stands watching, unobserved.*] Good heavens!

MRS. AUSTIN. You can't tell. You may have better success than you look for.

JIM. No . . . there's nothing can help me. I'm for the scrap heap.

MRS. AUSTIN. [*Eagerly.*] Wait and see. You are a man . . . you can be helped yet . . .

AUSTIN. [*Coming forward.*] What does this mean?

JIM. [*Starts wildly and reaches for revolver.*] Ha!

AUSTIN. [*Raising weapon.*] Hold up your hands!

MRS. AUSTIN. [*Rushing forward.*] No. Stop!

AUSTIN. What do you mean?

MRS. AUSTIN. I say stop! I promised him his freedom!

AUSTIN. My dear . . .

MRS. AUSTIN. Give me the weapon.

AUSTIN. Why . . .

MRS. AUSTIN. Give it to me. [*Takes revolver.*] Now sit down.

JIM. [*Has been staring wildly at* AUSTIN.] My God, it's the lawyer fellow!

MRS. AUSTIN. Yes, it is he.

AUSTIN. What does all this mean?

MRS. AUSTIN. Look at this man!

AUSTIN. [*Staring.*] Why?

MRS. AUSTIN. Don't you know him?

AUSTIN. No.

MRS. AUSTIN. Look carefully. [*Turns up light.*] Have you never seen him before?

AUSTIN. Never that I can recall. What is his name?
MRS. AUSTIN. I don't know. [*To* JIM.] What is it?
JIM. Humph! [*Hesitating.*] He could find out, anyway. Jim Faraday.
AUSTIN. Faraday . . . it sounds familiar.
JIM. [*Grimly.*] You've served the trick on a good many, I guess.
AUSTIN. [*To* MRS. AUSTIN.] What does he mean?
JIM. Don't you remember the Sisters' Hospital? The fellow that had his eye burned out in the big explosion?
AUSTIN. [*Startled.*] Oh!
JIM. [*Sneeringly.*] Ah, yes!
AUSTIN. You are the man?
JIM. I'm the man.
MRS. AUSTIN. Harvey, you took this man some paper to sign.
AUSTIN. Yes . . . I remember
MRS. AUSTIN. Did you tell him what was in it?
AUSTIN. [*Hesitates.*] Why . . .
MRS. AUSTIN. Answer me, please.
AUSTIN. Why, my dear . . .
MRS. AUSTIN. Did you tell him what was in it?
AUSTIN. But, my dear, it wasn't my business to tell him.
MRS. AUSTIN. Oh!
AUSTIN. I was representing the company.
MRS. AUSTIN. I see.
AUSTIN. It was his place to see what was in it.
MRS. AUSTIN. Harvey! This man with one eye burned out, and not yet over the accident?
AUSTIN. My dear, you don't understand . . .
JIM. [*Wildly.*] You didn't leave me to find out for myself. You lied to me!
MRS. AUSTIN. At least you permitted him to be misled.

You did not tell him the honest truth about the paper, and what would be the effect if he signed it.

AUSTIN. My dear, you do not understand. I could not have done that. I was the representative of the interests of the company.

MRS. AUSTIN. And that is the sort of work you do for them?

AUSTIN. That is the sort of work that has to be done. I cannot help it, much as I would like to . . .

MRS. AUSTIN. [*Wildly.*] You have done that sort of thing before. And you will do it again!

AUSTIN. My dear . . .

MRS. AUSTIN. And you take money for it! You bring that money home to me! And you never told me how you got it! You make me sharer in your guilt!

AUSTIN. Helen!

MRS. AUSTIN. This was how you earned your promotion! This was what you came to me and boasted about! This was what we married on. This money . . . blood money . . . that you get for cheating this helpless laborer out of his rights . . . out of everything he had in the world!

AUSTIN. My dear, you are out of your mind. You do not understand business.

MRS. AUSTIN. I understand it all . . . a child could understand! It is only you . . . the rising young lawyer . . . that doesn't understand! Harvey, Harvey! Do you know what you have done to this man . . . what you and I together have done to him? We have wrecked his life! We have driven him to hell! We have murdered his wife and his two children. We have turned him into a tramp and a criminal. We have climbed to success on top of him . . . we have made our fortune out of his blood! This house . . . this furniture . . . these pictures . . . all this beauty and comfort . . . all this we have coined out of his tears and agony . . . out of the lives of his sick wife and his two little babies! And you have done this for me . . . you have made me the cause of it . . . you have put the guilt of it upon my young life . . . a thing that I must carry through the world with me until I die!

AUSTIN. [*Starting toward her.*] Helen!

MRS. AUSTIN. No! Don't touch me! Speak to *him!* It is with him you have to do! What have you to say to him? Don't think about me!

AUSTIN. My dear, be reasonable!

MRS. AUSTIN. What have you to say to him? That is what I want to know! Harvey! Don't you understand it is your character that is up for judgment?

AUSTIN. It can't be as bad as you say.

MRS. AUSTIN. Why can't it? Find out.

AUSTIN. [*After a long pause, turns to* JIM.] Faraday.

JIM. Well?

AUSTIN. Is what my wife says true?

JIM. It's true.

AUSTIN. You got no damages from the company?

JIM. Didn't you fix it yourself? What do they pay you for?

AUSTIN. And had you no money saved?

JIM. My family had to live on it.

AUSTIN. And didn't you get your job back?

JIM. Until the shut-down, I did.

AUSTIN. Oh, that's so. I forgot that.

JIM. Humph!

AUSTIN. That's too bad. I will have to do something for you.

JIM. Will that bring my wife and babies back to life?

AUSTIN. Oh, your family died! My God . . . that's terrible! [*A pause.*] Faraday, I can't help that. What can I do? Listen, man . . . you see how unhappy my wife is . . . you don't want to make the thing impossible for me, do you?

JIM. I ain't doing anything.

AUSTIN. Be reasonable, and let me atone for the mistake. We'll say nothing about this . . . about to-night. We'll start over, and I'll see that you get a good job, and a fair chance.

JIM. Humph!

AUSTIN. Will you do that? I'm honestly sorry about it. And perhaps if I can give you some money for a start . . .

Takes out purse.

JIM. Put up your money. It ain't likely you've got as much there as I'd have got from the company.

AUSTIN. Oh, is that it? Well, maybe that is fair. I'll fix it up with you on that basis.

JIM. And what about the other fellows, hey?

AUSTIN. The other fellows?

JIM. That you've done out the same way you done me. What about Dan Kearney, that lost his life the day after . . . and you and the rest of the company sharks fixed it up so that his widow couldn't prove how it was that he got hurt!

MRS. AUSTIN. Harvey!

JIM. Yes, ma'am, they done that. And it ain't the first time they done it, either . . . nor the last. And they've bought juries . . . and judges, too, I reckon . . . there ain't much work of a dirty sort that the Empire Steel Company ain't tried in this city . . . and you can bet their smart young lawyers know all the game! I'm sorry for you, lady . . . you're white, and I'd be glad to help you. But I've seen too much of the company and its ways, and I won't lie down and lick its hand . . . not for any money! I ain't so low I've got the value of my wife and two little babies figured out and ready to hand. I reckon I'll stay on the outside of the fence and take my chances. I'll wind up in jail, I suppose; but there's many a better man than me done the same. So I guess I'll go, and we'll call it off.

Starts away.

MRS. AUSTIN. Harvey!

AUSTIN. My dear . . .

MRS. AUSTIN. Is that all you can say to him? You will let him go? [*To* JIM.] Listen to me. You are right. We can never undo what we have done. We cannot repay you. But at least we must do what we can. We cannot let the evil go on. You yourself have no right to do it . . . you have no right to give up your life.

JIM. I see what you mean, lady; and I'm sorry for you. I'd help you if I could. But it's too late . . . I know that. There can't anybody save me. I'm rotten . . . I'm a boozer. I couldn't stop if I wanted to. And I ain't got any reason to want to. I ain't in the running.

MRS. AUSTIN. [*Stretching out her arms.*] But what can I do?

JIM. You can look after them that ain't down. Look after them that your husband and the rest of the company's sharks will do up to-morrow.

MRS. AUSTIN. No!

JIM. Oh, they'll do it! I know what you mean . . . you'll make him stop . . . but they'll have another man in his place. It's a machine . . . it goes right on. Yes, and you won't do as much as you think you will, either . . . you'll think it over, and you won't go as far as you mean to now.

MRS. AUSTIN. No! No!

JIM. Ah, but you can't help it . . . you're in the mill, too. It's the class you belong to. You can talk and feel sorry . . . but you ain't made to do things. You have to have your houses and your fine dresses . . . and you couldn't live without them, and there'd be no use your trying. And that means you have to live off my class . . . you have to ride on our backs. And it don't much matter which part you ride on, as far as I can see. You'll make your husband get a new job, maybe; but he'll do the same thing in another way . . . only you won't find it out. But any way he gets his money it'll come out of me and my kind. D'ye see? I do the work . . . I'm the man underneath. I make the good things, and you get them. [*A pause.*] Good luck to you.

MRS. AUSTIN. You are cruel.

JIM. Nothing of the kind. I've just told you the facts. I feel sorry for you. I'd do anything I could for you. [*Stretching out his hands.*] See what I've done! I've given you your husband's life.

MRS. AUSTIN. Oh!

JIM. Yes, just that. You've no idea how many times I swore it . . . that I'd kill him on sight . . . that I'd strangle the life out of him, if ever I laid eyes on him again. I used to sit when I was half drunk, and brood over it . . . my God, I even swore it by the body of my little boy! And I've got my gun, and you've taken his away from him. And I don't shoot him. [*A pause.*] I leave him to you. [*Grimly.*] You punish him.

Exit right.

AUSTIN *stretches out his arms to his wife. She sinks upon the table, burying her head.*

CURTAIN

PRINCE HAGEN

CHARACTERS

(In order of appearance)

GERALD ISMAN: a poet.
MIMI: a Nibelung.
ALBERICH: King of the Nibelungs.
PRINCE HAGEN: his grandson.
MRS. ISMAN.
HICKS: a butler.
MRS. BAGLEY-WILLIS: mistress of Society.
JOHN ISMAN: a railroad magnate.
ESTELLE ISMAN: his daughter.
PLIMPTON: the coal baron.
RUTHERFORD: lord of steel.
DE WIGGLESTON RIGGS: cotillon leader.
LORD ALDERDYCE: seeing America.
CALKINS: Prince Hagen's Secretary.
NIBELUNGS; members of Society.

ACT I

SCENE 1. Gerald Isman's tent in Quebec.
SCENE 2. The Hall of State in Nibelheim.

ACT II

Library in the Isman home on Fifth Avenue: two years later.

ACT III

Conservatory of Prince Hagen's palace on Fifth Avenue. The wind-up of the opening ball: four months later.

ACT IV

Living room in the Isman camp in Quebec: three months later.

PRINCE HAGEN

ACT I

SCENE I

Shows a primeval forest, with great trees, thickets in background, and moss and ferns underfoot. A set in the foreground. To the left is a tent, about ten feet square, with a fly. The front and sides are rolled up, showing a rubber blanket spread, with bedding upon it; a rough stand, with books and some canned goods, a rifle, a fishing-rod, etc. Toward centre is a trench with the remains of a fire smoldering in it, and a frying pan and some soiled dishes beside it. There is a log, used as a seat, and near it are several books, a bound volume of music lying open, and a violin case with violin. To the right is a rocky wall, with a cleft suggesting a grotto.

At rise: GERALD *pottering about his fire, which is burning badly, mainly because he is giving most of his attention to a bound volume of music which he has open. He is a young man of twenty-two, with wavy auburn hair; wears old corduroy trousers and a grey flannel shirt, open at the throat. He stirs the fire, then takes violin and plays the Nibelung theme with gusto.*

GERALD. A plague on that fire! I think I'll make my supper on prunes and crackers to-night!
Plays again.

MIMI. [*Enters left, disguised as a pack-peddler; a little wizened up man, with long, unkempt grey hair and beard, and a heavy bundle on his back.*] Good evening, sir!

GERALD. [*Starts.*] Hello!

MIMI. Good evening!

GERALD. Why . . . who are you?

MIMI. Can you tell me how I find the road, sir?

GERALD. Where do you want to go?

MIMI. To the railroad.

GERALD. Oh, I see! You got lost?

MIMI. Yes, sir.

GERALD. [*Points.*] You should have turned to the right down where the roads cross.

MIMI. Oh. That's it!

Puts down burden and sighs.

GERALD. Are you expecting to get to the railroad to-night?

MIMI. Yes, sir.

GERALD. Humph! You'll find it hard going. Better rest. [*Looks him over, curiously.*] What are you—a peddler?

MIMI. I sell things. Nice things, sir. You buy?

Starts to open pack.

GERALD. No. I don't want anything.

MIMI. [*Gazing about.*] You live here all alone?

GERALD. Yes . . . all alone.

MIMI. [*Looking off left.*] Who lives in the big house?

GERALD. That's my father's camp.

MIMI. Humph! Nobody in there?

GERALD. The family hasn't come up yet.

MIMI. Why don't you live there?

GERALD. I'm camping out—I prefer the tent.

MIMI. Humph! Who's your father?

GERALD. John Isman's his name.

MIMI. Rich man, hey?
GERALD. Why . . . yes. Fairly so.
MIMI. I see people here last year.
GERALD. Oh! You've been here before?
MIMI. Yes. I been here. I see young lady. Very beautiful!
GERALD. That's my sister, I guess.
MIMI. Your sister. What you call her?
GERALD. Her name's Estelle.
MIMI. Estelle! And what's your name?
GERALD. I'm Gerald Isman.
MIMI. Humph! [*Looking about, sees violin.*] You play music, hey?
GERALD. Yes.
MIMI. You play so very bad?
GERALD. [*Laughs.*] Why . . . what makes you think that?
MIMI. You come 'way off by yourself!
GERALD. Oh! I see! No . . . I like to be alone.
MIMI. I hear you playing . . . nice tune.
GERALD. Yes. You like music?
MIMI. Sometimes. You play little quick tune . . . so? *Hums.*
GERALD. [*Plays Nibelung theme.*] This?
MIMI. [*Eagerly.*] Yes. Where you learn that?
GERALD. That's the Nibelung music.
MIMI. Nibelung music! Where you hear it?
GERALD. Why . . . it's in an opera.
MIMI. An opera?
GERALD. It's by a composer named Wagner.
MIMI. Where he hear it?
GERALD. [*Laughs.*] Why . . . I guess he made it up.
MIMI. What's it about? Hey?
GERALD. It's about the Nibelungs.
MIMI. Nibelungs?

GERALD. Queer little people who live down inside the earth, and spend all their time digging for gold.

MIMI. Ha! You believe in such people?

GERALD. [*Amused.*] Why . . . I don't know . . .

MIMI. You ever see them?

GERALD. No . . . but the poets tell us they exist.

MIMI. The poets, hey? What they tell you about them?

GERALD. Well, they have great rocky caverns, down in the depths of the earth. And they have treasures of gold . . . whole caves of it. And they're very cunning smiths . . . they make all sorts of beautiful golden vessels and trinkets.

MIMI. Trinkets, hey! [*Reaches into bundle.*] Like this, hey?

Holds up a gold cup.

GERALD. [*Surprised.*] Oh!

MIMI. Or this, hey?

GERALD. Why . . . where did you get such things?

MIMI. Ha, ha! You don't know what I got!

GERALD. Let me see them.

MIMI. You think the Nibelungs can beat that, hey? [*Reaches into bag.*] Maybe I sell you this cap! [*Takes out a little cap of woven gold chains.*] A magic cap, hey?

GERALD. [*Astounded.*] Why . . . what is it?

MIMI. [*Puts it on his head.*] You wear it . . . so. And you play Nibelung music, and you vanish from sight . . . nobody finds you. Or I sell you the magic ring . . . you wear that . . . [*Hands it to* GERALD.] Put it on your finger . . . so. Now you play, and the Nibelungs come . . . they dance about in the woods . . . they bring you gold treasures . . . ha, ha, ha! [*Amused at* GERALD's *perplexity.*] What you think they look like, hey? . . . those Nibelungs!

GERALD. Why . . . I don't know . . .

ACT I] **PRINCE HAGEN** 161

MIMI. What do your poets tell you? ha?
GERALD. Why . . . they're little men . . . with long hair and funny clothes . . . and humpbacked.
MIMI. Look like me, hey?
GERALD. [*Embarrassed.*] Why . . . yes . . . in a way.
MIMI. What are their names?
GERALD. Their names?
MIMI. Yes . . . what ones do you know about?
GERALD. Well, there was Alberich, the king.
MIMI. Alberich!
GERALD. He was the one who found the Rheingold. And then there was Hagen, his son.
MIMI. Hagen!
GERALD. He killed the hero, Siegfried.
MIMI. Yes, yes!
GERALD. And then there was Mimi.
MIMI. Ah! Mimi!
GERALD. He was a very famous smith.
MIMI. [*Eagerly.*] You know all about them! Somebody has been there!
GERALD. What do you mean?
MIMI. Would you like to see those Nibelungs?
GERALD. [*Laughing.*] Why . . . I wouldn't mind.
MIMI. You would like to see them dancing in the moonlight, and hear the clatter of their trinkets and shields? You would like to meet old King Alberich, and Mimi the smith? You would like to see that cavern yawn open . . . [*points to right*] and fire and steam break forth, and all the Nibelungs come running out? Would you like that? ha?
GERALD. Indeed I would!
MIMI. You wouldn't be afraid?
GERALD. No, I don't think so.
MIMI. But are you sure?
GERALD. Yes . . . sure!

MIMI. All right! You wear my magic ring! You wait till night comes! Then you play! [*Puts away trinkets.*] I must go now.

GERALD. [*Perplexed.*] What do you want for your ring?

MIMI. It is not for sale. I give it.

GERALD. What!

MIMI. Money could not buy it. [*Takes up pack.*] I came to you because you play that music.

GERALD. But I can't . . . it . . .

MIMI. It is yours . . . you are a poet! [*Starts left.*] Is this the way?

GERALD. Yes. But I don't like to . . .

MIMI. Keep it! You will see! Good-bye!

GERALD. But wait!

MIMI. It is late. I must go. Good-night.

Exit left.

GERALD. Good-night. [*Stands staring.*] Well, I'll be switched! If that wasn't a queer old customer! [*Looks at ring.*] It feels like real gold! [*Peers after* MIMI.] What in the world did he mean, anyhow? The magic ring! I hope he doesn't get lost in those woods to-night. [*Turns to fire.*] Confound that fire! It's out for good now! Let it go. [*Sits, and takes music score.*] Nibelungs! They are realer than anybody guesses. People who spend their lives in digging for gold, and know and care about nothing else. How many of them I've met at mother's dinner parties! Well, I must get to my work now. [*Makes a few notes; then looks up and stretches.*] Ah, me! I don't know what makes me so lazy this evening. This strange heaviness! There seems to be a spell on me. [*Gazes about.*] How beautiful these woods are at sunset! If I were a Nibelung, I'd come here for certain! [*Settles himself, re   ing; shadows begin to fall; music from orchestra.*] I'   ood for nothing but dreaming . . . I wish Estelle were here to sing to me! How **magical** the twilight is! Estelle! Estelle!

> *He lies motionless; music dies away, and there is a long silence. The forest is dark, with gleams of moonlight. Suddenly there is a faint note of music . . . the Nibelung theme. After a silence it is repeated; then again. Several instruments take it up. It swells louder. Vague forms are seen flitting here and there. Shadows move.*

GERALD. [*Starting up suddenly.*] What's that? [*Silence; then the note is heard again, very faint. He starts. It is heard again, and he springs to his feet.*] What's that? [*Again and again. He runs to his violin, picks it up, and stares at it. Still the notes are heard, and he puts down the violin, and runs down stage, listening.*] Why, what can it mean? [*As the music grows louder his perplexity and alarm increase. Suddenly he sees a figure stealing through the shadows, and he springs back, aghast.*] Why, it's a Nibelung! [*Another figure passes.*] Oh! I must be dreaming! [*Several more appear.*] Nibelungs! Why, it's absurd! Wake up, man! You're going crazy! [*Music swells louder; figures appear, carrying gold shields, chains, etc., with clatter.*] My God!

> *He stands with hands clasped to his forehead, while the uproar swells louder and louder, and the forms become more numerous. He rushes down stage, and the Nibelungs surround him, dancing about him in wild career, laughing, screaming, jeering. They begin to pinch his legs behind his back, and he leaps here and there, crying out. Gradually they drive him toward the grotto, which opens before them, revealing a black chasm, emitting clouds of steam. They rush in and are enveloped in the . Sounds of falling and crashing are heard The steam spreads, gradually veiling the front the stage.*

Nets rise with the steam, giving the effect of a descent. During this change the orchestra plays the music between Scenes II and III in Das Rheingold.

SCENE II

Nibelheim: a vast rocky cavern. Right centre is a large gold throne, and to the right of that an entrance through a great tunnel. Entrances from the sides also. At the left is a large golden vase upon a stand, and near it lie piles of golden utensils, shields, etc. Left centre is a heavy iron door, opening into a vault. Throughout this scene there is a suggestion of music, rising into full orchestra at significant moments. The voices of the Nibelungs are accompanied by stopped trumpets and other weird sounds.

At rise: The stage is dark. A faint light spreads. A company of Nibelungs crosses from right to left, carrying trinkets and treasures. Clatter of shields, crack of whips, music, etc. Another company of Nibelungs runs in left.

FIRST NIB. [*Entering.*] The earth-man has come!
SECOND NIB. Where is he?
FIRST NIB. He is with Mimi!
SECOND NIB. What is he like?
FIRST NIB. He is big! [*With a gesture of fright.*] Terrible!
THIRD NIB. Ah!
SECOND NIB. And the king? Does he know?
FIRST NIB. He has been told.
THIRD NIB. Where is the king?
FIRST NIB. He comes! He comes!

The orchestra plays the Fasolt and Fafnir music,

Rheingold, Scene II. Enter a company of Nibelungs, armed with whips, and marching with a stately tread. They post themselves about the apartment. Enter another company supporting KING ALBERICH. *He is grey-haired and very feeble, but ferocious-looking, and somewhat taller than the others. His robe is lined with ermine, and he carries a gold Nibelung whip—a short handle of gold, with leather thongs. He seats himself upon the throne, and all make obeisance. A solemn pause.*

ALBERICH. The earth-man has come?
FIRST NIB. Yes, your majesty!
ALB. Where is Mimi?
ALL. Mimi! Mimi!
The call is repeated off.
MIMI. [*Enters left.*] Your majesty.
ALB. Where is the earth-man?
MIMI. He is safe, your majesty.
ALB. Did he resist?
MIMI. I have brought him, your majesty.
ALB. And Prince Hagen? Has he come?
MIMI. He is without, your majesty.
ALB. Let him be brought in.
All cry out in terror.
MIMI. Your majesty. He is wild! He fights with everyone! He . . .
ALB. Let him be brought in.
ALL. Prince Hagen! Prince Hagen!
MIMI. [*Calling.*] Prince Hagen!
Some run out. The call is heard off. All stand waiting in tense expectation. The music plays the Hagen motives, with suggestions of the Siegfried funeral march. Voices are heard in the distance, and at the climax of the music PRINCE HAGEN *and his keepers enter. He is small for a man, but larger*

than any of the Nibelungs; a grim, sinister figure, with black hair, and a glowering look. His hands are chained in front of him, and eight Nibelungs march as a guard. He has bare arms and limbs, and a rough black bearskin flung over his shoulders. He enters right, and stands glaring from one to another.

ALB. Good evening, Hagen.

HAGEN. [*After a pause.*] Well?

ALB. [*Hesitating.*] Hagen, you are still angry and rebellious?

HAGEN. I am!

ALB. [*Pleading.*] Hagen, you are my grandson. You are my sole heir . . . the only representative of my line. You are all that I have in the world!

HAGEN. Well?

ALB. You place me in such a trying position! Have you no shame . . . no conscience? Why, some day you will be king . . . and one cannot keep a king in chains!

HAGEN. I do not want to be in chains!

ALB. But, Hagen, your conduct is such . . . what can I do? You have robbed . . . you have threatened murder! And you . . . my grandson and my heir . . .

HAGEN. Have you sent for me to preach at me again?

ALB. Hagen, this stranger . . . he has come to visit us from the world above. These earth-men know more than we . . . they have greater powers . . .

He hesitates.

HAGEN. What is all that to me?

ALB. You know that you yourself are three-quarters an earth-man . . .

HAGEN. I know it. [*With a passionate gesture.*] But I am in chains!

ALB. There may be a way of your having another chance. Perhaps this stranger will teach you. If you will promise to obey him, he will stay with you . . . he will be your tutor, and show you the ways of the earth-men.

HAGEN. No!
ALB. What?
HAGEN. I will not have it!
ALB. Hagen!
HAGEN. I will not have it, I say! Why did you not consult me?
ALB. But what is your objection . . .
HAGEN. I will not obey an earth-man! I will not obey anyone!
ALB. But he will teach you . . .
HAGEN. I do not want to be taught. I want to be let alone! Take off these chains!
ALB. [*Half rising.*] Hagen! I insist . . .
HAGEN. Take them off, I say! You cannot conquer me . . . you cannot trick me!
ALB. [*Angrily.*] Take him away!
The Nibelungs seize hold of him to hustle him off.
HAGEN. I will not obey him! Mark what I say . . . I will kill him. Yes! I will kill him!
He is dragged off protesting.
ALB. [*Sits, his head bowed with grief, until the uproar dies away; then, looking up.*] Mimi!
MIMI. Yes, your majesty.
ALB. Let the earth-man be brought.
MIMI. Yes, your majesty!
ALL. The earth-man! The earth-man!
The call is heard as before. GERALD *is brought on; the orchestra plays a beautiful melody, violins and horns.* MIMI *moves left to meet him.*
GERALD. [*Enters left with attendants; hesitating, gazing about in wonder. He sees* MIMI, *and stops; a pause.*] The pack peddler!

MIMI. The pack peddler!
GER. And these are Nibelungs?
MIMI. You call us that.
GER. [*Laughing nervously.*] You . . . er . . . it's a little disconcerting, you know. I had no idea you existed. May I ask your name?
MIMI. I am Mimi.
GER. Mimi! Mimi, the smith? And may I ask . . . are you real, or is this a dream?
MIMI. Is not life a dream?
GER. Yes . . . but . . .
MIMI. It is a story. You have to pretend that it is true.
GER. I see!
MIMI. You pretend that it is true . . . and then you see what happens! It is very interesting!
GER. Yes . . . I have no doubt. [*Peers at him.*] And just to help me straighten things out . . . would you mind telling me . . . are you old or young?
MIMI. I am young.
GER. How young?
MIMI. Nine hundred years young.
GER. Oh! And why did you come for me?
MIMI. The king commanded it.
GER. The king? And who may this king be?
MIMI. King Alberich.
GER. Alberich. [*Stares at the king.*] And is this he?
MIMI. It is he.
GER. And may I speak to him?
MIMI. You may.
ALB. Let the earth-man advance. Hail!
GER. Good evening, Alberich.
MIMI. [*At his elbow.*] Your majesty!
GER. Good evening, your majesty.

ALB. [*After a long gaze.*] You play our music. Where did you learn it?

GER. Why ... it's in Wagner's operas. He composed it.

ALB. Humph ... composed it!

GER. [*Aghast.*] You mean he came and copied it!

ALB. Of course!

GER. Why ... why ... we all thought it was original!

ALB. Original! It is indeed wonderful originality! To listen in the Rhine-depths to the song of the maidens, to dwell in the forest and steal its murmurs, to catch the crackling of the fire and the flowing of the water, the galloping of the wind and the death march of the thunder ... and then write it all down for your own! To take our story and tell it just as it happened ... to take the very words from our lips, and sign your name to them! Originality!

GER. But, your majesty, one thing at least. Even his enemies granted him that! He invented the invisible orchestra!

ALB. [*Laughing.*] Have you seen any orchestra here?

Siegfried motive sounds.

GER. I hadn't realized it! Do you mean that everything here happens to music?

ALB. If you only had the ears to hear, you would know that the whole world happens to music.

GER. [*Stands entranced.*] Listen! Listen!

ALB. It is very monotonous, when one is digging out the gold. It keeps up such a wheezing and pounding.

Stopped trumpets from orchestra.

GER. Ah, don't speak of such things! [*Gazes about; sees cup.*] What is this?

ALB. That is the coronation cup.

GER. The coronation cup?

ALB. One of the greatest of our treasures. It is worth

over four hundred thousand dollars. It is the work of the elder Mimi, a most wonderful smith.

GER. [*Advancing.*] May I look at it?

ALB. You will observe the design of the Rhine maidens.

GER. I can't see it here. It's too dark. Let me have a candle.

MIMI. A candle?

ALL. A candle!

ALB. My dear sir! Candles are so expensive! And why do you want to see it? We never look at our art treasures.

GER. Never look at them!

ALB. No. We know what they are worth, and everyone else knows; and what difference does it make how they look?

GER. Oh, I see!

ALB. Perhaps you would like to see our vaults of gold? [*Great excitement among the Nibelungs. The music makes a furious uproar.* ALBERICH *gives a great key to* MIMI, *who opens the iron doors.*] Approach, sir.

MIMI. Hear the echoes. [*Shouts.*]

GER. It must be a vast place!

ALB. This particular cavern runs for seventeen miles under the earth.

GER. What! And you mean it is all full of gold?

ALB. From floor to roof with solid masses of it.

GER. Incredible! Is it all of the Nibelung treasure?

ALB. All? Mercy, no! This is simply my own, and I am by no means a rich man. The extent of some of our modern fortunes would simply exceed your belief. We live in an age of enormous productivity. [*After a pause.*] Will you see more of the vault?

GER. No, I thank you. [*They close it.*] It must be getting late; and, by the way, your majesty, you know that no one has told me yet why you had me brought here.

ALB. Ah, yes, sure enough. We have business to talk about. Let us get to it! [*To* MIMI.] Let the hall be cleared. [MIMI *drives out the Nibelungs and retires.*] Sit on this rock here beside me. [*Confidentially.*] Now we can talk things over. I trust you are willing to listen to me.

GER. Most certainly. I am very much interested.

ALB. Thank you. You know, my dear sir, that I had a son, Hagen, who was the slayer of the great hero, Siegfried?

GER. Yes, your majesty.

ALB. A most lamentable affair. You did not know, I presume, that Hagen, too, had a son, by one of the daughters of earth?

GER. No. He is not mentioned in history.

ALB. That son, Prince Hagen, is now living; and, in the course of events, he will fall heir to the throne I occupy.

GER. I see.

ALB. The boy is seven or eight hundred years old, which, in your measure, would make him about eighteen. Now, I speak frankly. The boy is wild and unruly. He needs guidance and occupation. And I have sent for you because I understand that you earth-people think more and see farther than we do.

GER. Yes?

ALB. I wish to ask you to help me . . . to use your strength of mind and body to direct this boy.

GER. But what can I do?

ALB. I wish you to stay here and be Prince Hagen's tutor.

GER. What?

ALB. [*Anxiously.*] If you will do it, sir, you will carry hence a treasure such as the world has never seen before. And it is a noble work . . . a great work, sir. He is the grandson of a king! Tell me . . . will you help me?

Gazes imploringly.

GER. Let me think. [*A pause.*] Your majesty, I have things of importance to do, and I have no time to stay here . . .

ALB. But think of the treasures!

GER. My father is a rich man, and I have no need of treasures. And besides, I am a poet. I have work of my own . . .

ALB. Oh! don't refuse me, sir!

GER. Listen! There is, perhaps, something else we can do. How would it do to take Prince Hagen up to the world?

ALB. [*Starting.*] Oh!

GER. This world is a small one. There he might have a wide field for his energies. He might be sent to a good school, and taught the ideals of our Christian civilization.

ALB. [*Pondering anxiously.*] You mean that you yourself would see to it that proper care was given to him?

GER. If I took him with me it would mean that I was interested in his future.

ALB. It is a startling proposition. What opportunity can you offer him?

GER. I am only a student myself. But my father is a man of importance in the world.

ALB. What does he do?

GER. He is John Isman. They call him the railroad king.

ALB. You have kings in your world, also!

GER. [*Smiling.*] After a fashion . . . yes.

ALB. I had not thought of this. I hardly know what to reply. [*He starts.*] What is that?

An uproar is heard off left. Shouts and cries; music rises to deafening climax. Nibelungs flee on in terror.

HAGEN. [*Rushes on, struggling wildly, and dragging several Nibelungs.*] Let me go, I say! Take off these chains!

ALB. [*Rising in seat.*] Hagen!

HAGEN. I will not stand it, I tell you!

ALB. Hagen! Listen to me!

HAGEN. No!

ALB. I have something new to tell you. The earth-man has suggested taking you up with him to the world.

HAGEN. [*A sudden wild expression flashes across his features.*] No! [*He gazes from one to the other, half beside himself.*] You can't mean it!

ALB. It is true, Hagen.

HAGEN. What . . . why . . .

ALB. You would be sent to school and taught the ways of the earth-men. Do you think that you would like to go?

HAGEN. [*Wildly.*] By the gods! I would!

ALB. [*Nervously.*] You will promise to obey . . .

HAGEN. I'll promise anything! I'll do anything!

ALB. Hagen, this is a very grave decision for me. It is such an unusual step! You would have to submit yourself to this gentleman, who is kind enough to take charge of you . . .

HAGEN. I will! I will! Quick! [*Holding out his chains.*] Take them off!

ALB. [*Doubtfully.*] We can trust you?

HAGEN. You can trust me! You'll have no trouble. Take them off!

ALB. Off with them!

MIMI. [*Advances and proceeds to work at chains with a file.*] Yes, your majesty.

HAGEN. [*To* GERALD.] Tell me! What am I to do?

GER. You are to have an education . . .

HAGEN. Yes? What's it like? Tell me more about the earth-people.

GER. It's too much to try to tell. You will be there soon.

HAGEN. Ah! Be quick there! [*Tears one hand free and waves it.*] By the gods!

ALB. [*To* GERALD.] You had best spend the night with us and consult with me . . .

HAGEN. No, no! No delay! What's there to consult about?

ALB. We have so much to settle . . . your clothes . . . your money . . .

HAGEN. Give me some gold . . . that will be all. Let us be off!

GER. I will attend to everything. There is no need of delay.

HAGEN. Come on! [*Tears other hand free.*] Aha! [*Roams about the stage, clenching his hands and gesticulating, while the music rises to a tremendous climax.*] Free! Free forever! Aha! Aha! [*Turning to* GERALD.] Let us be off.

GER. All right. [*To* ALBERICH.] Good-bye, your majesty.

ALB. [*Anxiously.*] Good-bye.

HAGEN. Come on!

ALB. [*As Nibelungs gather about, waving farewell.*] Take care of yourself! Come back to me!

HAGEN. Free! Free! Ha, ha, ha!

MIMI. [*With Nibelungs.*] Good-bye!

ALB. Good-bye!

GER. Good-bye!

HAGEN. Free!

> *Exit, with* GERALD, *amid chorus of farewells, and wild uproar of music.*

CURTAIN

ACT II

Scene shows the library in a Fifth Avenue mansion; spacious and magnificent. There are folding doors right centre. There is a centre table with a reading lamp and books, and soft leather chairs. The walls are covered with bookcases. An entrance right to drawing-room. Also an entrance left.

At rise: GERALD, *in evening clothes, reading in front of fire.*

GER. [*Stretching, and sighing.*] Ah, me! I wish I'd stayed at the club. Bother their dinner parties!

MRS. IS. [*Enters right, a nervous, fussy little woman, in evening costume.*] Well, Gerald . . .

GER. Yes, mother?

MRS. IS. You're not coming to dinner?

GER. You don't need me, mother. You've men enough, you said.

MRS. IS. I like to see something of my son now and then.

GER. I had my lunch very late, and I'm honestly not hungry. I'd rather sit and read.

MRS. IS. I declare, Gerald, you run this reading business into the ground. You cut yourself off from everyone.

GER. They don't miss me, mother.

MRS. IS. To-night Rénaud is going to give us some crabflake à la Dewey! I told Mrs. Bagley-Willis I'd show her what crabflake could be. She is simply green with envy of our chef.

GER. I fancy that's the reason you invite her, isn't it?
MRS. IS. [*Laughs.*] Perhaps.
  Exit right. He settles himself to read.
HICKS. [*Enters centre.*] Mr. Gerald.
GER. Well?
HICKS. There was a man here to see you some time ago, sir.
GER. A man to see me? Why didn't you let me know?
HICKS. I started to, sir. But he disappeared, and I can't find him, sir.
GER. Disappeared? What do you mean?
HICKS. He came to the side entrance, sir; and one of the maids answered the bell. He was such a queer-looking chap that she was frightened, and called me. And then I went to ask if you were in, and he disappeared. I wasn't sure if he went out, sir, or if he was still in the house.
GER. What did he look like?
HICKS. He was a little chap . . . so high . . . with a long beard and a humped back . . .
GER. [*Startled.*] Mimi!
HICKS. He said you knew him, sir.
GER. Yes! I would have seen him.
HICKS. I didn't know, sir . . .
GER. Watch out for him. He'll surely come back.
HICKS. Yes, sir. I'm very sorry, sir.
  Exit centre.
GER. [*To himself.*] Mimi! What can that mean?
MIMI. [*Opens door, left, and peeps in.*] Ha!
GER. [*Starts.*] Mimi!
MIMI. Ssh!
GER. What is it?
MIMI. Where is Prince Hagen?
GER. I don't know.
MIMI. You don't know?
GER. No.

MIMI. But I must see him!
GER. I've no idea where he is.
MIMI. But . . . you promised to take care of him!
GER. Yes . . . and I tried to. But he ran away . . .
MIMI. What?
GER. I've not heard of him for two years now.
MIMI. [*Coming closer.*] Tell me about it.
GER. I took him to a boarding school . . . a place where he'd be taken care of and taught. And he rebelled . . . he would not obey anyone . . . [*Takes some faded telegrams from pocket book.*] See! This is what I got.
MIMI. What are they?
GER. Telegrams they sent me. [*Reads.*] Hagen under physical restraint. Whole school disorganized. Come immediately and take him away.
MIMI. Ha!
GER. That's one. And here's the other: Hagen has escaped, threatening teachers with revolver. Took train for New York. What shall we do? [*Puts away papers.*] And that's all.
MIMI. All?
GER. That was over two years ago. And I've not heard of him since.
MIMI. But he must be found!
GER. I have tried. I can't.
MIMI. [*Vehemently.*] But we cannot do without him!
GER. What's the matter?
MIMI. I cannot tell you. But we must have him! The people need him!
GER. He has lost himself in this great city. What can I do?
MIMI. He must be found. [*Voices heard centre.*] What is that?
GER. It is some company.

MIMI. [*Darts left.*] We must find Prince Hagen! He must come back to Nibelheim!
    Exit left.
MRS. BAGLEY-WILLIS. [*Off centre.*] It was crabflake à la Dewey she promised me!
    Enters with ISMAN.
GER. How do you do, Mrs. Bagley-Willis?
MRS. B.-W. How do you do, Gerald?
GER. Hello, father!
ISMAN. Hello, Gerald!
MRS. B-W. Am I the first to arrive?
GER. I think so.
MRS. B.-W. And how is Estelle after her slumming adventure?
GER. She's all right.
ISMAN. That was a fine place for you to take my daughter!
MRS. B.-W. It wasn't my fault. She would go. And her mother consented.
GER. I wish I'd been there with you.
MRS. B.-W. Indeed, I wished for someone. I was never more frightened in my life.
ISMAN. Did you see this morning's *Record?*
MRS. B.-W. No. What?
ISMAN. About that fellow, Steve O'Hagen?
MRS. B.-W. Good heavens!
GER. Nothing about Estelle, I hope!
ISMAN. No . . . apparently nobody noticed that incident. But about his political speech, and the uproar he's making on the Bowery. They say the streets were blocked for an hour . . . the police couldn't clear them.
GER. He must be an extraordinary talker.
MRS. B.-W. You can't imagine it. The man is a perfect demon!
GER. Where does he come from?

ISMAN. Apparently nobody knows. The papers say he turned up a couple of years ago . . . he won't talk about his past. He joined Tammany Hall, and he's sweeping everything before him.

GER. What do you suppose will come of it?

ISMAN. Oh, he'll get elected . . . what is it he's to be . . . an alderman? . . . and then he'll sell out, like all the rest. I was talking about it this afternoon, with Plimpton and Rutherford.

MRS. B.-W. They're to be here to-night, I understand.

ISMAN. Yes. . . so they mentioned. Ah! Here's Estelle!

ESTELLE. [*Enters, centre, with an armful of roses.*] Ah! Mrs. Bagley-Willis! Good evening!

MRS. B.-W. Good evening, Estelle.

EST. Good evening, father. Hello, Gerald.

GER. My, aren't we gorgeous to-night!

EST. Just aren't we!

MRS. B.-W. The adventure doesn't seem to have hurt you. Where is your mother?

GER. She went into the drawing-room. [MRS. B.-W. *and* ISMAN *go off, right;* ESTELLE *is about to follow.*] Estelle!

EST. What is it?

GER. What's this I hear about your adventure last night?

EST. [*With sudden seriousness.*] Oh, Gerald! [*Comes closer.*] It was a frightful thing! I've hardly dared to think about it!

GER. Tell me.

EST. Gerald, that man was talking straight at me . . . he meant every bit of it for me!

GER. Tell me the story.

EST. Why, you know, Lord Alderdyce had heard about this wild fellow, Steve O'Hagen, who's made such a sensation this campaign. And he's interested in our elections, and wanted to hear O'Hagen speak. He said he had a friend who'd arrange for us to be introduced to him; and so we went down there. And there was a most frightful crowd . . . it was an outdoor meeting, you know. We pushed our way into a saloon, where the mob was shouting around this O'Hagen. And then he caught sight of us . . . and Gerald, from the moment he saw me he never took his eyes off me! Never once!

GER. [*Smiling.*] Well, Estelle . . . you've been looked at before.

EST. Ah, but never like that!

GER. What sort of a man is he?

EST. He's small and dark and ugly . . . he wore a rough reefer and cap . . . but Gerald, he's no common man! There's something strange and terrible about him . . . there's a fire blazing in him. The detective who was with us introduced us to him . . . and he stood there and stared at me! I tried to say something or other . . . "I've been so interested in your speech, Mr. O'Hagen." And he laughed at me . . . "Yes, I've no doubt." And then suddenly . . . it was as if he leaped at me! He pointed his finger straight into my face, and his eyes fairly shone. "Wait for me! I'll be with you! I'm coming to the top!"

GER. Good God!

EST. Imagine it! I was simply paralyzed! "Mark what I tell you," he went on . . . "it'll be of interest to you some day to remember it. You may wait for me! I'm coming! You will not escape me!"

GER. Why . . . he's mad!

EST. He was like a wild beast. Everybody in the place was staring at us as he rushed on. "You have joy and power and freedom . . . all the privileges of life . . . all things that are excellent and beautiful. You are born to them . . . you claim them! And you come down here to stare at us as you might at some strange animals in a cage. You chatter and laugh and go your way . . . but remember what I told you . . . I shall be with you! You cannot keep *me* down! I shall be master of you all!"

GER. Incredible!

EST. And then in a moment it was all over. He made a mocking bow to the party . . . "It has given me the greatest pleasure in the world to meet you!" And with a wild laugh he went out of the door . . . and the crowd in the street burst into a roar that was like a clap of thunder. [*A pause.*] Gerald, what do you think he meant?

GER. My dear, you've been up against the class-war. It's rather the fashion now, you know.

EST. Oh, but it was horrible! I can't get it out of my mind. We heard some of his speech afterwards . . . and it seemed as if every word of it was meant for me! He lashed the crowd to a perfect fury . . . I think they'd have set fire to the city if he'd told them to. What do you suppose he expects to do?

GER. I can't imagine, I'm sure.

EST. I should like to know more about him. He was never raised in the slums, I feel certain.

GER. Steve O'Hagen. The name sounds Irish.

EST. I don't think he's Irish. He's dark and strange-looking . . . almost uncanny.

GER. I shall go down there and hear him the first chance I get. And now, I guess I'd best get out, if I want to dodge old Plimpton.

EST. Yes . . . and Rutherford, too. Isn't it a bore! I think they are perfectly odious people.

GER. Why do you suppose mother invited them?

EST. Oh, it's a business affair . . . they have forced their way into some deal of father's, and so we have to cultivate them.

GER. Plimpton, the coal baron! And Rutherford, the steel king! I wonder how many hundred millions of dollars we shall have to have before we can choose our guests for something more interesting than their Wall Street connections!

EST. I think I hear them. [*Listens.*] Yes . . . the voice. [*Mocking* PLIMPTON'S *manner and tone.*] Good evening, Miss Isman. I guess I'll skip it!

Exit right.

GER. And I, too!

Exit left.

RUTHERFORD. [*A stout and rather coarse-looking man, enters, right, with* PLIMPTON.] It's certainly an outrageous state of affairs, Plimpton!

PLIMPTON. [*A thin, clerical-looking person, with square-cut beard.*] Disgraceful! Disgraceful!

RUTH. The public seems to be quite hysterical!

PLIMP. We have got to a state where simply to be entrusted with great financial responsibility is enough to constitute a man a criminal; to warrant a newspaper in prying into the intimate details of his life, and in presenting him in hideous caricatures.

RUTH. I can sympathize with you, Plimpton . . . these government investigations are certainly a trial. [*Laughing.*] I've had my turn at them . . . I used to lie awake nights trying to remember what my lawyers had told me to forget!

PLIMP. Ahem! Ahem! Yes . . . a rather cynical jest! I can't say exactly . . .

MRS. IS. [*In doorway, right.*] Ah, Mr. Plimpton! How do you do? And Mr. Rutherford?

PLIMP. Good evening, Mrs. Isman.

RUTH. Good evening, Mrs. Isman.

MRS. IS. You managed to tear yourself away from business cares, after all!

PLIMP. It was not easy, I assure you.

MRS. IS. Won't you come in?

RUTH. With pleasure.
Exit, right, with MRS. ISMAN, *followed by* PLIMPTON.
GER. [*Enters, left.*] That pious old fraud! [*Sits in chair.*] Well, I'm safe for a while!
Sprawls at ease and reads.
HICKS. [*Enters, centre.*] A gentleman to see you, Mr. Gerald.
GER. Hey? [*Takes card, looks, then gives violent start.*] Prince Hagen! [*Stands aghast, staring; whispers, half dazed.*] Prince Hagen!
HICKS. [*After waiting.*] What shall I tell him, sir?
GER. What . . . what does he look like?
HICKS. Why . . . he seems to be a gentleman, sir.
GER. How is he dressed?
HICKS. For dinner, sir.
GER. [*Hesitates, gazes about nervously.*] Bring him here . . . quickly!
HICKS. Yes, sir.
GER. And shut the door afterwards.
HICKS. Yes, sir.
Exit.
GER. [*Stands staring.*] Prince Hagen! He's come at last!
Takes the faded telegrams from his pocket; looks at them; then goes to door, right, and closes it.
HICKS. [*Enters, centre.*] Prince Hagen.
HAGEN. [*Enters; serene and smiling, immaculately clad.*] Ah, Gerald!
GER. [*Gazing.*] Prince Hagen!
HAGEN. You are surprised to see me!
GER. I confess that I am.
HAGEN. Did you think I was never coming back?
GER. I had given you up.
HAGEN. Well, here I am . . . to report progress.

GER. [*After a pause.*] Where have you been these two years?

HAGEN. Oh, I've been seeing life . . .

GER. You didn't like the boarding school?

HAGEN. [*With sudden vehemence.*] Did you think I would like it? Did you think I'd come to this world to have my head stuffed with Latin conjugations and sawdust?

GER. I had hoped that in a good Christian home . . .

HAGEN. [*Laughing.*] No, no, Gerald! I let you talk that sort of thing to me in the beginning. It sounded fishy even then, but I didn't say anything . . . I wanted to get my bearings. But I hadn't been twenty-four hours in that good Christian home before I found out what a kettleful of jealousies and hatreds it was. The head master was an old sap-head; and the boys! . . . I was strange and ugly, and they thought they could torment and bully me; but I fought 'em . . . by the Lord, I fought 'em day and night, I fought 'em all around the place! And when I'd mastered 'em, you should have seen how they cringed and toadied! They hated the slavery they lived under, but not one of them dared raise his hand against it.

GER. Well, you've seen the world in your own way. Now are you ready to go back to Nibelheim?

HAGEN. Good God, no!

GER. You know it's my duty to send you back.

HAGEN. Oh, say! My dear fellow!

GER. You know the solemn promise I made to King Alberich.

HAGEN. Yes . . . but you can't carry it out.

GER. But I can!

HAGEN. How?

GER. I could invoke the law, if need be. You know you are a minor . . .

HAGEN. My dear boy, I'm over seven hundred years old!

GER. Ah, but that is a quibble. You know that in our world that is only equal to about eighteen . . .

HAGEN. I have read up the law, but I haven't found any provision for reducing Nibelung ages to your scale.

GER. But you can't deny . . .

HAGEN. I wouldn't need to deny. The story's absurd on the face of it. You know perfectly well that there are no such things as Nibelungs! [GERALD *gasps.*] And besides, you're a poet, and everybody knows you're crazy. Fancy what the newspaper reporters would do with such a yarn! [*Cheerfully.*] Come, old man, forget about it, and let's be friends. You'll have a lot more fun watching my career. And besides, what do you want? I've come back, and I'm ready to follow your advice.

GER. How do you mean?

HAGEN. You told me to stay in school until I'd got my bearings in the world. And then I was to have a career. Well, I've got my education for myself . . . and now I'm ready for the career. [*After a pause.*] Listen, Gerald. I said I'd be a self-made man. I said I'd conquer the world for myself. But of late I've come to realize how far it is to the top, and I can't spare the time.

GER. I see.

HAGEN. And then . . . besides that . . . I've met a woman.

GER. [*Startled.*] Good heavens!

HAGEN. Yes. I'm in love.

GER. But surely . . . you don't expect to marry!

HAGEN. Why not? My mother was an earth-woman, and her mother, also.

GER. To be sure. I'd not realized it. [*A pause.*] Who is the woman?

HAGEN. I don't know. I only know she belongs in

this world of yours. And I've come to seek her out. I shall get her, never fear!

GER. What are your plans?

HAGEN. I've looked this Christian civilization of yours over . . . and I'm prepared to play the game. You can take me up and put me into Society . . . as you offered to do before. You'll find that I'll do you credit.

GER. But such a career requires money.

HAGEN. Of course. Alberich will furnish it, if you tell him it's needed. You must call Mimi.

GER. Mimi is here now.

HAGEN. [*Starting.*] What!

GER. He is in the house.

HAGEN. For what?

GER. He came to look for you.

HAGEN. What is the matter?

GER. I don't know. He wants you to return to Nibelheim.

HAGEN. Find him. Let me see him!

GER. All right. Wait here.
   Exit left.

HAGEN. What can that mean?

EST. [*Enters, right. sees* PRINCE HAGEN, *starts wildly and screams.*] Ah! [*She stands transfixed; a long pause.*] Steve O'Hagen! [*A pause.*] Steve O'Hagen! What does it mean?

HAGEN. Who are you?

EST. I live here.

HAGEN. Your name?

EST. Estelle Isman.

HAGEN. [*In a transport of amazement.*] Estelle Isman! You are Gerald's sister!

EST. Yes.

HAGEN. By the gods!

EST. [*Terrified.*] You know my brother!

HAGEN. Yes.
EST. You . . . Steve O'Hagen!
HAGEN. [*Gravely.*] I am Prince Hagen!
EST. Prince Hagen!
HAGEN. A foreign nobleman.
EST. What . . . what do you mean? You were on the Bowery!
HAGEN. I came to this country to study its institutions. I wished to know them for myself . . . therefore I went into politics. Don't you see?
EST. [*Dazed.*] I see!
HAGEN. Now I am on the point of giving up the game and telling the story of my experiences.
EST. What are you doing here . . . in this house?
HAGEN. I came for you.
EST. [*Stares at him.*] How *dare* you?
HAGEN. I would dare anything for you! [*They gaze at each other.*] Don't you understand?
EST. [*Vehemently.*] No! No! I am afraid of you! You have no business to be here!
HAGEN. [*Taking a step towards her.*] Listen . . .
EST. No! I will not hear you! You cannot come here!
Stares at him, then abruptly exit, centre.
HAGEN. [*Laughs.*] Humph! [*Hearing voices.*] Who is this?
RUTH. [*Off right.*] I don't agree with you.
IS. Nor I, either, Plimpton. [*Enters with* PLIMPTON *and* RUTHERFORD; *sees* HAGEN.] Oh . . . I beg your pardon.
HAGEN. I am waiting for your son, sir.
IS. I see. Won't you be seated?
HAGEN. I thank you. [*Sits at ease in chair.*]
PLIM. My point is, it's as Lord Alderdyce says . . . we have no hereditary aristocracy in this country, no traditions of authority . . . nothing to hold the mob in check.

IS. There is the constitution.
PLIM. They may over-ride it.
IS. There are the courts.
PLIM. They may defy the courts.
RUTH. Oh, Plimpton, that's absurd!
PLIM. Nothing of the kind, Rutherford! Suppose they were to elect to office some wild and reckless demagog . . . take, for instance, that ruffian you were telling us about . . . down there on the Bowery . . . [HAGEN *starts, and listens*] and he were to defy the law and the courts? He is preaching just that to the mob . . . striving to rouse the elemental wild beast in them! And some day they will pour out into this avenue . . .

RUTH. [*Vehemently.*] Very well, Plimpton! Let them come! Have we not the militia and the regulars? We could sweep the avenue with one machine gun . . .

PLIM. But suppose the troops would not fire?
RUTH. But that is impossible!
PLIM. Nothing of the kind, Rutherford! No, no . . . we must go back of all that! It is in the hearts of the people that we must erect our defenses. It is the spirit of this godless and skeptical age that is undermining order. We must teach the people the truths of religion. We must inculcate lessons of sobriety and thrift, of reverence for constituted authority. We must set our faces against these new preachers of license and infidelity . . . we must go back to the old-time faith . . . to love, and charity, and self-sacrifice . . .

HAGEN. [*Interrupting.*] That's it! You've got it there!
IS. [*Amazed.*] Why . . .
PLIM. Sir?
HAGEN. You've said it! Set the parsons after them! Teach them heaven! Set them to singing about harps and golden crowns, and milk and honey flowing! Then you can shut them up in slums and starve them, and they

won't know the difference. Teach them non-resistance and self-renunciation! You've got the phrases all pat . . . handed out from heaven direct! Take no thought saying what ye shall eat! Lay not up for yourselves treasures on earth! Render unto Cæsar the things that are Cæsar's!

IS. Why . . . this is preposterous!

PLIM. This is blasphemy!

HAGEN. You're Plimpton . . . Plimpton, the coal baron, I take it. I know you by your pictures. You shut up little children by tens of thousands to toil for you in the bowels of the earth. You crush your rivals, and form a trust, and screw up prices to freeze the poor in winter! And you . . . [*to* RUTHERFORD] you're Rutherford, the steel king, I take it. You have slaves working twelve hours a day and seven days a week in your mills. And you mangle them in hideous accidents, and then cheat their widows of their rights . . . and then you build churches, and set your parsons to preach to them about love and self-sacrifice! To teach them charity, while you crucify justice! To trick them with visions of an imaginary paradise, while you pick their pockets upon earth! To put arms in their hands, and send them to shoot their brothers, in the name of the Prince of Peace!

RUTH. This is outrageous!

PLIM. [*Clenching his fists.*] Infamous scoundrel!

RUTH. [*Advancing upon* HAGEN.] How dare you!

HAGEN. It stings, does it? Ha! Ha!

PLIM. [*Sputtering.*] You wretch!

IS. This has gone too far. Stop, Rutherford! Calm yourself, Plimpton. Let us not forget ourselves! [*To* PRINCE HAGEN, *haughtily.*] I do not know who you are, sir, or by what right you are in my house. You say that you are a friend of my son's . . .

HAGEN. I claim that honor, sir.

IS. The fact that you claim it prevents my ordering

you into the street. But I will see my son, sir, and find out by what right you are here to insult my guests. [*Turning.*] Come, Plimpton. Come, Rutherford . . . we will bandy no words with him!

They go off, centre.

HAGEN. [*Alone.*] By God! I touched them! Ha, ha, ha! [*Grimly.*] He will order me into the street! [*With concentrated fury.*] That is it! They shut you out! They build a wall about themselves! Aristocracy! [*Clenching his fist.*] Very well! So be it! You sit within your fortress of privilege! You are haughty and contemptuous, flaunting your power! But I'll breach your battlements, I'll lay them in the dust! I'll bring you to your knees before me!

A silence. Suddenly there is heard, very faintly, the Nibelung theme. It is repeated; HAGEN *starts.*

MIMI. [*Enters, left.*] Prince Hagen!
HAGEN. Mimi!
MIMI. At last!
HAGEN. [*Approaching.*] What is it?
MIMI. [*Beckons.*] Come here.
HAGEN. [*In excitement.*] What do you want?
MIMI. You must come back!
HAGEN. What do you mean?
MIMI. The people want you.
HAGEN. What for?
MIMI. They need you. You must be king.
HAGEN. [*Wildly.*] Ha?
MIMI. Alberich . . .
HAGEN. Alberich?
MIMI. He is dead!
HAGEN. [*With wild start.*] Dead!
MIMI. Yes . . . he died last night!
HAGEN. [*Turns pale and staggers; then leaps at* MIMI, *clutching him by the arm.*] No! No!

MIMI. It is true.

HAGEN. My God! [*A look of wild, drunken rapture crosses his face; he clenches his hands and raises his arms.*] Ha, ha, ha!

MIMI. [*Shrinks in horror.*] Prince Hagen!

HAGEN. He is dead! He is *dead!* [*Leaps at* MIMI.] The gold?

MIMI. The gold is yours.

HAGEN. Ha, ha, ha! It is mine! It is mine! [*Begins pacing the floor wildly.*] Victory! *Victory!* VICTORY! Ha, ha, ha! Ha, ha, ha! [*Spreads out his arms, with a triumphant shout.*] I have them! By God! Isman! Plimpton and Rutherford! Estelle! I have them all! It is triumph! It is glory! It is the world! I am King! I am King! *King!* KING! [*Seizes* MIMI *and starts centre; the music rises to climax.*] To Nibelheim! To Nibelheim! [*Stands stretching out his arms in exultation; a wild burst of music.*] Make way for Hagen! *Make way for Hagen!*

CURTAIN

ACT III

The conservatory is a study in green and gold, with strange tropical plants having golden flowers. There are entrances right and left. In the centre, up-stage, is a niche with a gold table and a couple of gold chairs, and behind these a stand with the "coronation cup"; to the right the golden throne from Nibelheim, and to the left a gold fountain splashing gently.

At rise: The stage is empty. The strains of an orchestra heard from ball-room, left.

MRS. BAGLEY-WILLIS. [*Enters, right, with* DE WIGGLESTON RIGGS; *she wears a very low-cut gown, a stomacher and tiara of diamonds, and numerous ropes of pearls.*] Well, Wiggie, he has made a success of it!

DE WIGGLESTON RIGGS. [*Petit and exquisite.*] He was certain to make a success when Mrs. Bagley-Willis took him up!

MRS. B.-W. But he wouldn't do a single thing I told him. I never had such a protégé in my life!

DE W. R. Extraordinary!

MRS. B.-W. I told him it would be frightfully crude, and it is. And yet, Wiggie, it's impressive, in its way . . . nobody can miss the feeling. Such barbaric splendor!

DE W. R. The very words! Barbaric splendor!

MRS. B.-W. I never heard of anything like it . . . the man simply poured out money. It's quite in a different class from other affairs.

DE W. R. [*Holding up his hands.*] Stupefying!

MRS. B.-W. And did you ever know the public to take such interest in a social event? People haven't even stopped to think about the panic in Wall Street.

DE W. R. I assure you, Mrs. Bagley-Willis, it begins a new epoch in our social history. [*To* LORD ALDERDYCE, *who enters, left, with* GERALD.] How do you do, Lord Alderdyce?

MRS. B.-W. Good evening, Lord Alderdyce. Good evening, Gerald.

LORD A. Good evening, Mrs. Bagley-Willis. Good evening, Mr. Riggs.

GERALD. Good evening, Wiggie! [DE W. R. *and* MRS. B.-W. *move toward left.*] I suppose that old lady's taken to herself all the credit for this evening's success!

LORD A. Well, really, you know, wasn't it . . . ah . . . quite a feat to make society swallow this adventurer?

GERALD. How can anybody stay away? When a man spends several millions on a single entertainment people have to come out of pure curiosity.

LORD A. To be sure! I did, anyway!

GER. [*Gazing about.*] Think of buying all the old Vandergrift palaces at one swoop!

LORD A. Oh, really!

GER. This palace was one of the landmarks of the city; all its decorations had been taken from old palaces in Italy. And he tore everything off and gave it away to a museum, and he made it over in three months!

LORD A. Amazing.

Music and applause heard left.

MRS. B.-W. Mazzanini must be going to sing again.

DE W. R. Let us go!

MRS. B.-W. Fancy opera stars to dance to! A waltz song at a thousand dollars a minute!

DE W. R. Ah, but *such* a song!

They go off, left; half a dozen guests enter, right, and cross in groups.

RUTH. [*Enters, right, with* PLIMPTON; *looking about.*] An extraordinary get-up!

PLIMP. Appalling extravagance, Rutherford! Appalling!

RUTH. Practically everybody's here.

PLIMP. Everybody I ever heard of.

RUTH. One doesn't meet you at balls very often, Plimpton.

PLIM. No. To tell the truth, I came from motives of prudence.

RUTH. Humph! To tell the truth, so did I!

PLIM. The man is mad, you know . . . and one can't tell what might offend him!

RUTH. And with the market in such a state!

PLIM. It's terrible! Terrible! . . . ah, Lord Alderdyce!

LORD A. Good evening, Mr. Plimpton. How d'ye do, Mr. Rutherford?

RUTH. As well as could be expected, Lord Alderdvce. It's a trying time for men of affairs.

They pass on, and go off, left.

GER. They must be under quite a strain just now.

LORD A. Don't mention it. Don't mention it! I've invested all my funds in this country, and I tremble to pick up the last edition of the paper!

MRS. IS. [*Enters, right, costumed en grande dame, much excited.*] Oh, Gerald, Lord Alderdyce, what do you think I've just heard?

LORD A. What?

MRS. IS. About Prince Hagen and Mrs. Bagley-Willis . . . how she came to take him up! Percy Pennington told me about it . . . he's her own first cousin, you know, Lord Alderdyce . . . and he vows he saw the letter in her desk!

LORD A. Oh, tell us!

MRS. IS. Well, it was just after Prince Hagen made his appearance, when the papers were printing pages about him. And the news came that he'd bought these palaces; and the next day Mrs. Bagley-Willis got a letter marked personal. Percy quoted the words . . . Dear Madam: I wish to enter Society. I have no time to go through with the usual formalities. I am a nobleman, with an extraordinary mind and unlimited money. I intend to entertain New York Society as it has never dreamed of being entertained before. I should be very pleased if you would co-operate with me in making my opening ball a success. If you are prepared to do this, I am prepared to pay you the sum of one million dollars cash as soon as I receive your acceptance. Needless to say, of course, this proposition is entirely confidential!

LORD. A. By jove!

MRS. IS. Think of it!

GER. But can it be true?

MRS. IS. What is more likely, my dear? You know that Mrs. Bagley-Willis has been spending millions every season to entertain at Newport; and their fortune will never stand that! Oh, I must give it to Van Tribber . . . he'll see that the papers have it!

LORD A. But hadn't you better make sure that it's really . . .

MRS. IS. It doesn't make the slightest difference! Everybody will know that it's true!

GER. They are ready to believe anything about Prince Hagen.

MRS. IS. Certainly, after a glimpse of this palace. Did you ever see such frantic money-spending in your life?

LORD A. Never!

MRS. IS. Gold! Gold! I am positively blinded with

the sight of gold. I'd seen every kind of decoration and furniture, I thought . . . but solid gold is new to me!

LORD A. Just look at this cup, for instance! [*Points to coronation cup.*] And those fountains . . . I believe that even the basins are of gold.

MRS. IS. Perhaps we could stop the water and see.

LORD A. I must go . . . I have a dance. I am sorry not to see your daughter.

MRS. IS. Yes . . . it was too bad she couldn't come. Good-bye.

LORD ALDERDYCE *exit*.

MRS. IS. [*Pointing to throne.*] Look at that thing, Gerald!

GER. Yes . . . no wonder the crowd came!

MRS. IS. I imagine a good many came because they didn't dare stay away. They certainly can't be enjoying themselves after such a day down town.

GER. It was too bad the panic should come just on the eve of the ball.

MRS. IS. My dear Gerald! That's his sense of humor! He wanted to bring them here and set them to dancing and grinning, while in their hearts they are frightened to death.

GER. How did he do it, anyway?

MRS. IS. Why, he seems to have money without limit . . . and he's been buying and buying . . . everything in sight! You know how prices have been soaring the past two months. And of course the public went wild, and took to speculating. Then Prince Hagen sold; and the bottom has simply dropped out of everything.

GER. I see. And do you suppose the slump has hit father?

MRS. IS. I don't know. He won't talk to me about it. But it's easy to see how distressed he is. And then, to cap the climax, Estelle refuses to come here! Prince Hagen is certain to be furious.

GER. For my part, I admire her courage.

MRS. IS. But, Gerald ... we can't afford to defy this man.

GER. Estelle can afford it, I hope.

MRS. IS. Here comes your father now. Look at him! Gerald, won't you go, please ... I want to have a talk with him.

GER. All right.

Exit, right.

MRS. IS. John!

ISMAN. [*Enters, left, pale and depressed.*] What is it?

MRS. IS. You look so haggard and worried!

IS. I *am* worried!

MRS. IS. You ought to be home in bed.

IS. I couldn't sleep. What good would it do?

MRS. IS. Aren't you going to get any rest at all?

IS. It's time for reports from the London markets pretty soon. They open at five o'clock, by our time. And I'm hoping there may be some support for Intercontinental ... it's my last hope!

MRS. IS. Oh, dear me! Dear me!

IS. If that fails, there is nothing left for us. We are ruined! Utterly ruined!

MRS. IS. John!

IS. We shall be paupers!

MRS. IS. John Isman, that's absurd! A man who's worth a hundred million dollars, like you ...

IS. It'll be gone ... all of it!

MRS. IS. Gone?

IS. Do you realize that to-day I had to sell every dollar of my Transatlantic stock?

MRS. IS. [*Horrified.*] Good God!

IS. There has never been a day like it in all history! There are no words to tell about it!

MRS. IS. Oh, that monster!

IS. And the worst of it is, the man seems to be after me particularly! Everything I rely upon seems to collapse . . . everywhere I turn I find that I'm blocked.

MRS. IS. Oh, it must have been because of that affair in our house . . . and in the saloon that dreadful night. We ought never to have gone to that place! I knew as soon as I laid eyes on the man that he'd do us harm.

IS. We must keep out of his power. We must save what we can from the wreck and learn to do with it. You'll have to give up your Newport plans this year.

MRS. IS. [*Aghast.*] *What!*

IS. We won't be able to open the house.

MRS. IS. You're mad!

IS. My dear . . .

MRS. IS. Now, John Isman, you listen to me! I was quite sure you had some such idea in your mind! And I tell you right now, I simply will not hear of it! I . . .

IS. But what can we do, my dear?

MRS. IS. I don't know what we can do! But you'll have to raise money somehow. I will not surrender my social position to Mrs. Bagley-Willis . . . not for all the Wall Street panics in the world. Oh, that man is a fiend! I tell you, John Isman . . .

IS. Control yourself!

HAGEN. [*Off right.*] Very well! I shall be charmed, I'm sure. [*Enters.*] Oh! How do you do, Mrs. Isman?

MRS. IS. Oh, Prince Hagen, a most beautiful evening you've given us.

HAGEN. Ah! I'm glad if you've enjoyed it.

MRS. IS. Yes, indeed . . .

IS. Prince Hagen, may I have a few words with you?

HAGEN. Why, surely . . . if you wish . . .

IS. I do.

MRS. IS. Prince Hagen will excuse me.
Exit, left.

HAGEN. [*Goes to table, centre, and sits opposite* ISMAN.] Well?

IS. Prince Hagen, what do you want with me?

HAGEN. [*Surprised.*] Why ... the pleasure of your company.

IS. I mean in the Street.

HAGEN. Oh! Have you been hit?

IS. Don't mock me. You have used your resources deliberately to ruin me. You have followed me ... you have taken every railroad in which I am interested, and driven it to the wall. And I ask you, man to man, what do you want?

HAGEN. [*After some thought.*] Isman, listen to me. You remember four months ago I offered you a business alliance?

IS. I had no idea of your resources then. Had I known, I should not have rejected your offer. Am I being punished for that?

HAGEN. No, Isman ... it isn't punishment. Had you gone into the alliance with me it would have been just the same. It was my purpose to get you into my power.

IS. Oh!

HAGEN. To bring you here ... to make you sit down before me, and ask, What do you want? ... And so I will tell you what I want, man to man! [*A pause.*] I want your daughter.

IS. [*Starts.*] What!

HAGEN. I want your daughter.

IS. Good God!

HAGEN. Do you understand now?

IS. [*Whispering.*] I understand!

HAGEN. Isman, you are a man of the world, and we

can talk together. I love your daughter, and I wish to make her my wife.

IS. And so you ruined me!

HAGEN. Four months ago I was an interloper and an adventurer. In a month or two I shall be the master of your financial and political world. Then I had nothing to offer your daughter. Now I can make her the first lady of the land.

IS. But, man, we don't sell our children ... not in America.

HAGEN. Don't talk to me like a fool, Isman. I never have anything to do with your shams.

IS. But the girl! She must consent!

HAGEN. I'll attend to that. Meantime, I want you to know what I mean. On the day that your daughter marries me I will put you at the head of my interests, and make you the second richest man in America. You understand?

IS. [*Weakly.*] I understand.

HAGEN. Very well. And don't forget to tell your wife about it. [*He rises.*]

IS. Is that all?

HAGEN. No; one thing more. Your daughter is not here to-night.

IS. No.

HAGEN. I wish her to come.

IS. But ... she is indisposed!

HAGEN. That is a pretext. She did not want to come.

IS. Possibly ...

HAGEN. Tell her to come.

IS. [*Startled.*] What? Now? It is too late!

HAGEN. Nonsense. Your home is only a block away. Telephone to her.

IS. [*Dismayed.*] But ... she will not be ready.

HAGEN. Tell her to come! Whatever she is wearing,

she will outshine them all. [ISMAN *hesitates a moment, as if to speak, then goes off, right, half dazed; the other watches him, laughing silently to himself.*] That's all right! [*Sees Calkins.*] Ah, Calkins!

CALKINS. [*Enters with an armful of papers.*] Here are the morning papers, Prince.

HAGEN. Ah! [*Takes them.*] Still moist! Did you think I wanted them that badly?

CAL. Promptness never harms.

HAGEN. [*Opening papers.*] That's true. Ah, they hardly knew which was more important . . . the ball or the panic! We filled them up pretty full. Did you see if they followed the proofs?

CAL. There are no material changes.

HAGEN. Ha! Ha! Cartoons! Prince Hagen invites the Four Hundred with one hand and knocks them down with the other! Pretty good! Pretty good! What's this? Three millions to decorate his palaces . . . half a million for a single ball?

CAL. I suppose they couldn't credit the figures.

HAGEN. Humph! We'll educate them! [*Sweeps papers out of the way.*] So much for that! Were all the orders for the London opening gone over?

CAL. All correct, Prince.

HAGEN. Very good! That's all. [CAL. *exit.*] They're all anxious about London . . . I can see it! Ah, Gerald!

GER. [*Enters, right.*] Hello!

HAGEN. [*Smiling.*] You see, they came to my party!

GER. Yes.

HAGEN. They smile and chatter . . . they bow and cringe to me . . . and I have not preached any of your Christian virtues, either!

GER. No. I grant it. It's a very painful sight. [*After a pause.*] That was a pleas* fancy . . . to have a panic on the eve of your ball!

HAGEN. It wasn't nearly as bad as I meant it to be. Wait and see to-day's!

GER. What's the end of it all?

HAGEN. The end? Why have an end? I didn't make this game . . . I play it according to other men's rules. I buy and sell stocks, and make what money I can. The end may take care of itself.

GER. It's rather hard on the helpless people, isn't it?

HAGEN. Humph! The people! [*After a pause.*] Gerald, this world of yours has always seemed to me like a barrel full of rats. There's only room for a certain number on top, and the rest must sweat for it till they die.

GER. It's not a very pleasant image to think of.

HAGEN. I don't think of it. I simply happen to find myself on top, and I stay there and enjoy the view. [*Seats himself at table.*] As a matter of fact, Gerald, one of the things I intend to do with this world is to clean it up. Don't imagine that I will tolerate such stupid waste as we have at present . . . everybody trying to cheat everybody else, and nobody to keep the streets clean. It's as if a dozen men should go out into a field to catch a horse, and spend all their time in trying to keep each other from catching it. When I take charge they'll catch the horse.

GER. [*Drily.*] And you'll ride him.

HAGEN. And I'll ride him.

Laughs.

GER. [*After a pause.*] At first I couldn't make out why you bothered with this Society game. Now I begin to understand. You wanted to see them!

HAGEN. I wanted to watch them wriggle! I wanted to take them, one by one, and strip off their shams! Take that fellow Rutherford, the steel man! Or Plimpton, the coal baron, casting his eyes up to heaven, and singing psalms through his nose! The instant I laid eyes on that whining old hypocrite, I hated him; and I vowed I'd never rest again till I'd shown him as he is . . . a coward and a knave! And I tell you, Gerald, before I get through with him . . . Ah, there he is!

PLIM. [*Off.*] Hello, Isman!

HAGEN. Come.

Draws back with GERALD.

IS. [*Entering, right, with* PLIMPTON *and* RUTHERFORD.] Any word yet?

PLIM. Nothing yet!

RUTH. Such a night as this has been!

IS. If the thing keeps up to-day the Exchange will have to close . . . there will be no help for it.

PLIM. We are in the hands of a madman!

RUTH. We must have a conference with him . . . we must find out what he wants.

IS. Did you speak to him, Plimpton?

PLIM. I tried to. I might as well have butted my head against a stone wall. "I have money," he said, "and I wish to buy and sell stocks. Isn't that my right?"

RUTH. He's a fiend! A fiend!

PLIM. He smiled as he shook my hand . . . and he knows that if coal stocks go down another ten points I'll be utterly ruined!

IS. Terrible! Terrible!

PLIM. [*To* RUTHERFORD.] Rutherford, have you learned any more about where his money comes from?

RUTH. I meant to tell you . . . I've had another report. The mystery deepens every hour. It's always the same thing . . . the man takes a train and goes out into the country; he gathers all the wagons for miles around, and goes to some place in the woods . . . and there is a pile of gold, fifty tons of it, maybe, covered over with brush. Nobody knows how it got there, nobody has time to ask. He loads it into the wagons, takes it aboard the train, and brings it to the Sub-treasury.

IS. The man's an alchemist! He's been manufacturing it and getting ready.

RUTH. Perhaps. Who can tell? All I know is the Sub-treasury has bought over two billion dollars' worth of gold bullion in the last four months . . . and what can we do in the face of that?

PLIM. No wonder that prices went up to the skies!

RUTH. I had the White House on the 'phone this afternoon. We can demonetize gold . . . the government can refuse to buy any more.

IS. But then what would become of credit?

PLIM. [*Vehemently.*] No, no . . . that will not help! [*Gazes about nervously.*] There's only one thing. [*Whispers.*] That man must be killed!

RUTH. [*Horrified.*] Ah!

IS. No.

PLIM. Just that! Nothing else will help! And instantly . . . or it will be too late.

IS. Plimpton!

PLIM. He must not be alive when the Exchange opens this morning!

RUTH. But how?

PLIM. I don't know . . . but we must find a way! We owe it as a public duty . . . the man is a menace to society. Rutherford, you are with me?

RUTH. By God! I am!

IS. You're mad!

PLIM. You don't agree with me?

IS. It's not to be thought of! You're forgetting yourself, Plimpton . . .

PLIM. [*Gazing about.*] This is no place to discuss it. But I tell you that if there is no support from London . . .

RUTH. [*Starting.*] Come . . . perhaps there may be

word! [*They start left.*] We may beat them yet . . . who can tell?

  PLIMPTON, RUTHERFORD *and* ISMAN *go off.*

HAGEN. [*Emerges with* GERALD *from shadows, shaking with laughter.*] Ha! ha! ha! Love and self-sacrifice! You see, Gerald!

GER. Yes . . . I see! [*Looks right . . . then starts violently.*] My sister!

HAGEN. Ah!

GER. What does this mean?

HAGEN. [*To* ESTELLE, *who enters, right, evidently agitated.*] Miss Isman!

EST. My father said . . .

HAGEN. Yes. Won't you sit down?

EST. [*Hesitatingly.*] Why . . . I suppose so . . .

HAGEN. [*To* GERALD.] Will you excuse us, please, Gerald?

GER. [*Amazed.*] Why, yes . . . but Estelle . . .

EST. [*In a faint voice.*] Please go, Gerald.

GER. Oh! very well.

  Exit, left.

EST. You wished to see me.

HAGEN. Yes. [*Sitting opposite.*] How do you like it all?

EST. It is very beautiful.

HAGEN. Do you really think so?

EST. [*Wondering.*] Don't you?

HAGEN. No.

EST. Truly?

HAGEN. No.

EST. Then why did you do it?

HAGEN. To please you.

EST. [*Shrinks.*] Oh!

HAGEN. [*Fixes his gaze on her, and slowly leans across*

table; with intensity.] Haven't you discovered yet that you are mine?

EST. [*Half rising.*] Prince Hagen!

HAGEN. How long will it be before you know it?

EST. How dare you?

HAGEN. Listen. I am a man accustomed to command. I have no time to play with conventions . . . I cannot dally and plead. But I love you. I cannot live without you! And I will shake the foundations of the world to get you!

EST. [*Staring, fascinated; whispers.*] Prince Hagen!

HAGEN. All this . . . [*waving his hand*] I did in the hope that it would bring you here . . . so that I might have a chance to tell you. Simply for that one purpose. I have broken the business world to my will . . . that also was to make you mine!

EST. [*Wildly.*] You have ruined my father!

HAGEN. Your father has played this game, and his path is strewn with the rivals he has ruined. He knows that, and you know it. Now *I* have played the game; and I have beaten him. It took me one day to bring him down . . . [*Laughs.*] It will take me less time to put him back again.

EST. But why, why?

HAGEN. Listen, Estelle. I came to this civilization of yours, and looked at it. It seemed to me that it was built upon knavery and fraud . . . that it was altogether a vile thing . . . rotten to the core of it! And I said I would smash it, as a child smashes a toy; I would toss it about . . . as your brother the poet tosses his metaphors. But then I saw you, and in a flash all that was changed. You were beautiful . . . you were interesting. You were something in the world worth winning . . . something I had not known about before. But you stood upon the pinnacle of Privilege . . . you gathered the clouds about your head. How should I climb to you?

EST. [*Frightened.*] I see!

HAGEN. I came to your home . . . I was turned from the door. So I set to work to break my way to you.

EST. I see!

HAGEN. And that is how I love you. You are all there is in the game to me. I bring the world and lay it at your feet. It is all yours. You do not like what I do with it, perhaps. Very well . . . take it and do better. The power is yours for the asking! Power without end! [*He reaches out his arms to her; a pause.*] You do not like my way of love-making, perhaps. You find me harsh and rude. But I love you. And where, among the men that you know, will you find one who can feel for you what I feel . . . who would dare for you what I have dared? [*Gazes at her with intensity.*] Take your time. I have no wish to hurry you. But you must know that, wherever you go, my hand is upon you. All that I do, I do for the love of you.

EST. [*Weakly.*] I . . . you frighten me!

HAGEN. All the world I lay at your feet! You shall see.

PLIM. [*Off left.*] Prince Hagen!

HAGEN. [*Starting.*] Ah!

PLIM. [*Enters, running, in great agitation, with a telegram.*] Prince Hagen!

HAGEN. Well?

PLIM. I have a report from London. The market has gone all to pieces!

HAGEN. Ah!

PLIM. Pennsylvania coal is down twenty-five points in the first half hour. I'm lost . . . everything is lost!

RUTH. [*Running on.*] Prince Hagen! Steel is down to four! And the Bank of England suspends payments! What . . .

PLIM. What do you want with us? What are you trying to do?

RUTH. [*Wildly.*] You've crushed us! We're helpless, utterly helpless!

PLIM. Have you no mercy? Aren't you satisfied when you've got us down?

RUTH. Are you going to ruin everybody? Are you a madman?

PLIM. What are you trying to do? What do you want?

HAGEN. [*Has been listening in silence. Suddenly he leaps into action, an expression of furious rage coming upon his face. His eyes gleam, and he raises his hand as if to strike the two.*] Get down on your knees!

PLIM. Ha!

RUTH. What?

HAGEN. [*Louder.*] Get down on your knees! [PLIMPTON *sinks in horror.* PRINCE HAGEN *turns upon* RUTHERFORD.] Down!

RUTH. [*Sinking.*] Mercy!

HAGEN. [*As they kneel before him, his anger vanishes; he steps back.*] There! [*Waving his hand.*] You asked me what I wanted? I wanted this . . . to see you there . . . upon your knees! [*To spectators, who appear right and left.*] Behold!

RUTH. Oh!

Starts to rise.

HAGEN. [*Savagely.*] Stay where you are! . . . To see you on your knees! To hear you crying for mercy, which you will not get! You pious plunderers! Devourers of the people! Assassins of women and helpless children! Who made the rules of this game . . . you or I? Who cast the halo of righteousness about it . . . who sanctified it by the laws of God and man? Property! Property was holy! Property must rule! You carved it into your constitutions . . . you taught it in your newspapers, you preached it from your pulpits! You screwed down wages, you screwed up prices ... it must be right, because it paid! Money was the test ... money was the end! You were business men! Practical men! Don't you know the phrases? Money talks! Business is business! The gold standard ... ha, ha, ha! The gold standard! Now someone has come who has more gold than you. You were masters ... now *I* am the master! And what you have done to the people I will do to you! You shall drink the cup that you have poured out for them ... you shall drink it to the dregs!

PLIM. [*Starting to rise.*] Monster!

HAGEN. Stay where you are! Cringe and grovel and whine! [*Draws a Nibelung whip from under his coat.*] I will put the lash upon your backs! I will strip your shams from you ... I will see you as you are! I will take away your wealth, that you have wrung from others! Before I get through with you you shall sweat with the toilers in the trenches! For I am the master now! *I* have the gold! *I* own the property! The world is mine! You were lords and barons ... you ruled in your little principalities! But I shall rule everywhere ... everything ... all civilization! I shall be king! King! [*With exultant gesture.*] Make way for the king! *Make way for the king!*

CURTAIN

ACT IV

The scene shows a spacious room, fitted with luxurious rusticity. To the right of centre are a couple of broad windows, leading to a veranda. In the corner, right is a table, with a telephone. In the centre of the room is a large table, with a lamp and books, and a leather arm-chair at each side. To the left of centre is a spacious stone fireplace, having within it a trap door opening downward. At the left a piano with a violin upon it. There are exposed oak beams; antlers, rifles, snowshoes, etc., upon the walls. Entrances right and left.

At rise: CALKINS, *standing by the desk, arranging some papers.*

CALKINS. [*As 'phone rings.*] Hello! Yes, this is the Isman camp. Prince Hagen is staying here. This is his secretary speaking. No, Prince Hagen does not receive telephone calls. No, not under any circumstances whatever. It doesn't make any difference. If the President of the United States has anything to say to Prince Hagen, let him communicate with Mr. Isman at his New York office, and the message will reach him. I am sorry . . . those are my instructions. Good-bye. [*To* HICKS, *who enters with telegram.*] Hicks, for the future, Prince Hagen wishes all messages for him to be taken to my office. That applies to letters, telegrams . . . everything.

HICKS. Very good, sir.

Exit.

CAL. [*Opening a telegram.*] More appeals for mercy.

HAGEN. [*Enters from veranda, wearing white flannels, cool and alert.*] Well, Calkins?
CAL. Nothing important, sir.
HAGEN. The market continues to fall?
CAL. Copper is off five points, sir.
HAGEN. Ah!
CAL. The President of the United States tried to get you on the 'phone just now.
HAGEN. Humph! Anything else?
CAL. There has been another mob on Fifth Avenue this morning. They seem to be threatening your palace.
HAGEN. I see. You wrote to the mayor, as I told you?
CAL. Yes, sir.
HAGEN. Well, you'd best put in another hundred guards. And they're to be instructed to shoot.
CAL. Yes, sir.
HAGEN. Let them be men we can depend on . . . I don't want any mistake about it. I don't care about the building, but I mean to make a test of it.
CAL. I'll see to it, sir.
HAGEN. Anything else?
CAL. A message from a delegation from the National Unemployment Conference. They are to call to-morrow morning.
HAGEN. Ah, yes. Make a note, please . . . I sympathize with their purpose, and contribute half a million. [*To* GERALD, *who enters, left.*] Hello, Gerald . . . how are you? Make yourself at home. [*To* CALKINS.] I attribute the present desperate situation to the anarchical struggles of rival financial interests. I am assuming control, and straightening out the tangle as rapidly as I can. The worst of the crisis is over . . . the opposition is capitulating, and I expect soon to order a general resumption of industry. Prepare me an address of five hundred words . . . sharp and snappy. Then see the head of the

delegation, and have it understood that the affair is not to occupy more than fifteen minutes.

CAL. Very good, sir.

HAGEN. And stir up our Press Bureau. We must have strong, conservative editorials this week . . . It's the crucial period. Our institutions are at stake . . . the national honor is imperilled . . . order must be preserved at any hazard . . . all that sort of thing.

CAL. Yes, sir . . . I understand.

HAGEN. Very good. That will be all.

CAL. Yes, sir.

Exit, right.

GER. You're putting the screws on, are you?

HAGEN. Humph! Yes. It's funny to hear these financial men . . . their one idea in life has been to dominate . . . and now they cry out against tyranny!

GER. I can imagine it.

HAGEN. Here's Plimpton, making speeches about American democracy! These fellows have got so used to making pretenses that they actually deceive themselves.

GER. I've noticed that you make a few yourself now.

HAGEN. Yes . . . don't I do it well? [*Thoughtfully.*] You know, Gerald, pretenses are the greatest device that your civilization had to teach me.

GER. Indeed?

HAGEN. We never made any pretenses in Nibelheim; and when I first met you, your talk about virtue and morality and self-sacrifice was simply incomprehensible to me. It seemed something quite apart from life. But now I've come to perceive that this is what makes possible the system under which you live.

GER. Explain yourself.

HAGEN. Here is this civilization . . . simply appalling in its vastness. The countless millions of your people, the wealth you have piled up . . . it seems like a huge bubble that may burst any minute. And the one device by which it is all kept together . . . is pretense!

GER. Why do you think that?

HAGEN. Life, Gerald, is the survival of the strong. I care not if it be in a jungle or in a city, it is the warfare of each against all. But in the former case it's brute force, and in the latter it's power of mind. And don't you see that the ingenious device which makes the animal of the slums the docile slave of the man who can outwit him . . . is this Morality . . . this absolutely sublimest invention, this most daring conception that ever flashed across the mind of man?

GER. Oh, I see.

HAGEN. I used to wonder at it down there on the Bowery. The poor are a thousand to your one, and the best that is might be theirs, if they chose to take it; but there is Morality! They call it their virtue. And so the rich man may have his vices in peace. By heaven, if that is not a wondrous achievement, I have not seen one!

GER. You believe this morality was invented by the rich.

HAGEN. I don't know. It seems to be a congenital disease.

GER. Some people believe it was implanted in man by God.

HAGEN. [*Shrugging his shoulders.*] Perhaps. Or by a devil. Men might have lived in holes, like woodchucks, and been fat and happy; but now they have Morality, and toil and die for some other man's delight.

CAL. [*Enters, right.*] Are you at leisure, sir?

HAGEN. Why?

CAL. Mr. Isman wants you on the 'phone.

HAGEN. Oh! All right . . .

Goes to 'phone.

GER. [*Rises.*] Perhaps I . . .

HAGEN. No, that's all right. [*Sits at 'phone.*] Hello! Is that Isman? How are you? [*To* CALKINS.] Calkins!
CAL. Yes, sir.
Sits and takes notes.
HAGEN. How about Intercontinental? [*Imperiously.*] But *I* can! I said the stock was to go to sixty-four, and I want it to go. I don't care what it costs, Isman . . . let it go in the morning . . . and don't ever let this happen again. I have sent word you are to have another hundred million by nine-thirty. Will that do? Don't take chances. Oh, Rutherford! Tell Rutherford my terms are that the directors of the Fidelity Life Insurance Company are to resign, and he is to go to China for six months. Yes. I mean that literally . . . Plimpton? What do I want with his banks . . . I've got my own money . . . And, oh, by the way, Isman . . . call up the White House again, and tell the President that the regulars will be needed in New York. . . . No, I understand you . . . I think I've fixed matters up at this end. I've got two hundred guards up here, and they're picked men . . . they'll shoot if there's need. I'm not talking about it, naturally . . . but I'm taking care of myself. You keep your nerve, Isman. It'll all be over in a month or two more . . . these fellows are used to having their own way, and they make a fuss. And, by the way, as to the newspapers . . . we'll turn out that paper trust crowd, and stop selling paper to the ones that are making trouble. That'll put an end to it, I fancy. You had best get after it yourself, and have it attended to promptly. You might think of little things like that yourself, Isman . . . no, you're all right; only you haven't got enough imagination. But just get onto this job, and let me hear that it's done before morning. Good-bye. [*Hangs up receiver.*] Humph! [*To* GERALD.] They've about got your father's nerve.
GER. I can't say that I blame him very much. [*In*

sombre thought.] Really, you know, Prince Hagen, this can't go on. What's to be the end of it?

HAGEN. [*Laughing.*] Oh, come, come, Gerald . . . don't bother your head with things like that! You're a poet . . . you must keep your imagination free from such dismal matters. . . . See, I've got a job for you. [*Pointing to books on table.*] Do you notice the titles?

GER. [*Has been handling the books absent-mindedly; now looks at titles.*] The Saints' Everlasting Rest. Pilgrim's Progress. The Life of St. Ignatius. . . . What does that mean?

HAGEN. I'm studying up on religion. I want to know the language.

GER. I see!

HAGEN. But I don't seem to get hold of it very well. I think it's the job for you.

GER. How do you mean?

HAGEN. I'm getting ready to introduce Morality into Nibelheim.

GER. What?

HAGEN. [*Playfully.*] You remember you talked to me about it a long time ago. And now I've come to your way of thinking. Suppose I gave you a chance to civilize the place, to teach those wretched creatures to love beauty and virtue?

GER. It would depend upon what your motive was in inviting me.

HAGEN. *My* motive? What has that to do with it? Virtue is virtue, is it not? . . . No matter what I think about it?

GER. Yes.

HAGEN. And virtue is its own reward?

GER. Perhaps so.

HAGEN. Let us grant that the consequences of educating and elevating the Nibelungs . . . of teaching them to love righteousness . . . would be that they were deprived of all their gold, and forced to labor at getting more for a wicked capitalist like me. Would it not still be right to teach them?

GER. It might, perhaps.

HAGEN. Then you will try it?

GER. No . . . I'm afraid not.

HAGEN. Why not?

GER. [*Gravely.*] Well . . . for one thing . . . I have weighty reasons for doubting the perfectibility of the Nibelungs.

HAGEN. [*Gazes at him; then shakes with laughter.*] Really, Gerald, that is the one clever thing I've heard you say!

GER. [*Laughing.*] Thank you!

HAGEN. [*Rises and looks at watch.*] Your mother was coming down. Ah! Mrs. Isman!

MRS. IS. [*Enters, left.*] Good afternoon, Prince Hagen.

HAGEN. And how go things?

MRS. IS. I've just had a telegram from my brother. He says that the Archbishop of Canterbury never goes abroad, and was shocked at the suggestion; but he thinks two million might fetch him.

HAGEN. Very well . . . offer it.

MRS. IS. Do you really think it's worth that?

HAGEN. My dear lady, it is worth anything if it will make you happy and add to the éclat of the wedding. There's nothing too good for Estelle.

MRS. IS. Ah, what a wonderful man you are. [*Eyeing him.*] I was wondering how rose pink would go with your complexion.

HAGEN. Dear me! Am I to wear rose pink?

MRS. IS. No, but I'm planning the decoration for the wedding breakfast. . . . And I'm puzzled about the flowers. I'm weary of orchids and la France roses . . . Mrs.

Bagley-Willis had her ball room swamped with them last week.

HAGEN. We must certainly not imitate Mrs. Bagley-Willis.

MRS. IS. [*Complacently.*] I fancy she's pretty nearly at the end of her rope. My maid tells me she couldn't pay her grocer's bill till she got that million from you!

HAGEN. Ha, ha, ha!

MRS. IS. I wish you'd come with me for a moment . . . I have some designs for the breakfast menu . . .

HAGEN. Delighted, I'm sure.

They go off, left.

GER. Oh, my God!

EST. [*Enters in a beautiful afternoon gown, and carrying an armful of roses; she is nervous and preoccupied.*] Ah! Gerald!

GER. Estelle.

He watches her in silence; she arranges flowers.

EST. How goes the poem, Gerald?

GER. The poem! Who could think of a poem at a time like this? [*Advancing toward her.*] Estelle! I can bear it no longer!

EST. What?

GER. This crime! I tell you it's a crime you're committing!

EST. Oh, Gerald! Don't begin that again. You know it's too late. And it tears me to pieces!

GER. I can't help it. I must say it!

EST. [*Hurrying toward him.*] Brother! You must not say another word to me! I tell you you must not . . . I can't bear it!

GER. Estelle . . .

EST. No, I say . . . no! I've given my word! My honor is pledged, and it's too late to turn back. I have permitted father to incur obligations before all the world

GER. But, Estelle, you don't know. If you understood all ... all ...

EST. [*With sudden intensity.*] Gerald! I know what you mean! I have felt it! You know more about Prince Hagen than you have told me. There is some secret—something strange. [*She stares at him wildly.*] I don't want to know it! Gerald ... don't you understand? We are in that man's hands! We are at his mercy! Don't you know that he would never give me up? He would follow me to the end of the earth! He would wreck the whole world to get me! I am in a cage with a wild beast!

They stare at each other.

GER. [*In sudden excitement.*] Estelle!

EST. What?

GER. Can it be that you love this man?

EST. [*Startled.*] I don't know! How can I tell? He terrifies me. He fascinates me. I don't know what to make of him. And I don't dare to think. [*Wildly.*] And what difference does it make? I have promised to marry him!

MRS. ISMAN *enters, left, and listens.*

EST. And I must keep my word! You must not try to dissuade me ...

MRS. IS. Estelle!

EST. Mother!

MRS. IS. Has Gerald been tormenting you again? My child, my child ... I implore you, don't let that madness take hold of you! Think of our position. [*Attempts to embrace her.*] I know how it is ... I went through with it myself. We women all have to go through with it. I did not care for your father ... it nearly broke my heart. I was madly in love at the time ... truly I was! But think what will become of us ...

EST. [*Vehemently, pushing her away.*] Mother! I forbid you to speak another word to me! I will not hear it! I will keep my bargain. I will do what I have said I will do. But I will not have you talk to me about it . . . Do you understand me?

MRS. IS. My dear!

EST. Please go! Both of you! I wish to be alone!

MRS. IS. [*In great agitation.*] Oh, dear me! dear me!
Exit, left.

GER. Good-bye!
Exit, right; ESTELLE *recovers herself by an effort; stands by table in thought. Twilight has begun to gather.*

HAGEN. [*Enters by veranda.*] Ah! Estelle! [*Comes toward her.*] My beautiful! [*Makes to embrace her.*] Not yet?

EST. [*Faintly.*] Prince Hagen, I told you . . .

HAGEN. I know, I know! But how much longer? I love you! The sight of you is fire in my veins. Have I not been patient? The time is very short . . . when will you let me . . .
Advances.

EST. [*Gasping.*] Give me . . . give me till to-morrow!

HAGEN. [*Gripping his hands.*] To-morrow! Very well! [*Turns to table.*] Ah, flowers! Do you like the new poppies?

EST. They are exquisite!

HAGEN. [*Sits in chair.*] Well, we've had a busy day to-day.

EST. Yes. You must be tired.

HAGEN. In your house? No!

EST. Rest, even so. [*Goes to piano.*] I will play for you. [*Sits, and takes Rheingold score.*] One of Gerald's scores.
Plays a little, then sounds the Nibelung theme.
PRINCE HAGEN *starts. She repeats it.*

HAGEN. No . . . no!

EST. Why—what's the matter?

HAGEN. That music! What is it?

EST. It's some of the Nibelung music. Gerald had it here.

HAGEN. Don't play it! [*Hesitating.*] Music jars on me now ... I've too much on my mind.

EST. [*Rising.*] Oh ... very well. It is time for tea, anyway. Have you talked with father to-day?

HAGEN. Three times. He is in the thick of the fight. He plays the game well.

EST. He has played it a long time.

HAGEN. Yes. [*'Phone rings.*] Ah! What is that? [*Takes receiver.*] Hello! Yes ... oh, Isman! I see! More trouble in Fifth Avenue, hey? Well, are the regulars there? Why don't they fire? Women and children in front! Do they expect to accomplish anything by that? No, don't call me up about matters like that, Isman. The orders have been given. No ... not an inch! Let the orders be carried out. That is all. Good-bye.

Hangs up receiver.

EST. [*Has been listening in terror.*] Prince Hagen!

HAGEN. Well?

EST. What does that mean?

HAGEN. It means that the slums are pouring into Fifth Avenue.

EST. [*A pause.*] What do they want?

HAGEN. Apparently they want to burn my palace.

EST. And the orders ... what are the orders?

HAGEN. The orders are to shoot, and to shoot straight.

EST. Is it for me that you are doing this?

HAGEN. How do you mean?

EST. You told me you brought all the world and laid it at my feet. Is this part of the process?

HAGEN. Yes, this is part.

EST. [*Stares at him intently; whispers.*] How do you do it?

HAGEN. What?

EST. What is the secret of your power? They are millions, and you are only one ... yet you have them bound! Is it some spell that you have woven? [*A pause;* HAGEN *stares at her. She goes on, with growing intensity and excitement.*] They are afraid of your gold! Afraid of your gold! All the world is afraid of it! It is nothing —it is a dream ... it is a nightmare! If they would defy you ... if they would open their eyes ... it would go as all nightmares go! But you have made them believe in it! They cower and cringe before it! They toil and slave for it! They take up arms and murder their brothers for it! They sell their minds and their souls for it! And all because no one dares to defy you! No one! No one! [*In a sudden transport of passion.*] *I* defy you! [PRINCE HAGEN *starts; she gazes at him wildly.*] I will not marry you! I will not sell myself to you! Not for any price that you can offer ... not for any threat that you can make! Not in order that my mother may plan wedding breakfasts and triumph over Mrs. Bagley-Willis! Not in order that my father may rule in Wall Street and command the slaughter of women and children! Nor yet for the fear of anything that you can do!

HAGEN. [*In a low voice.*] Have you any idea what I will do?

EST. [*Desperately.*] I know what you mean ... you have me at your mercy! You have your guards—I am in a trap! And you mean *force* ... I have felt it in all your actions ... behind all your words. Very well! There is a way of escape, even from that; and I will take it! You can compel me to kill myself; but you can never compel me to marry you! Not with all the power you can summon ... not with all the wealth of the world! Do you understand me? [*They stare at each other.*] I have heard you talk with my brother, and I know what are your ideas. You came to our civilization, and tried it, and found it a lie. Virtue and honor ... justice and mercy ... all these things were pretenses ... snares for the unwary. There was no one you could not frighten with your gold! That is your creed, and so far it has served you ... but no farther! There is one thing in the world you cannot get ... one thing that is beyond the reach of all your cunning! And that is a woman's soul. [*With a gesture of exultant triumph.*] You cannot buy me!

HAGEN. Estelle!

EST. *Go!*

HAGEN. [*Stretching out his arms to her.*] I love you!

EST. You *love* me! The slave driver ... with his golden whip!

HAGEN. Even so ... I love you.

EST. What do you know of love? What does the word mean to you? Before love must come justice and honor, with it come mercy and self-sacrifice ... all things that you deride and trample on. What have you to do with love?

HAGEN. [*With intensity.*] I love you! More than anything else in all the world ... I love you!

EST. [*Stares at him.*] More than your power?

HAGEN. Estelle! Listen to me! You do not know what my life has been! But I can say this for myself ... I have sought the best that I know. I have sought Reality. [*A pause.*] I seek your love! I seek those things which you have, and which I have not. [*Fiercely.*] Do you think that I have not felt the difference?

EST. [*In a startled whisper.*] No!

HAGEN. That which you have, and which I have not, has become all the world to me! I love you ... I cannot live without you. I will follow you wherever you command. Only teach me how to win your love.

EST. I cannot make terms with you. I will not hear of love from you while you have force in your hands.

HAGEN. I will leave your home. I will set you free. I will humble myself before you. What else can I do?

EST. You can lay down your power.

HAGEN. Estelle! Those are mere words.

EST. No!

HAGEN. Who is to take up the power? Shall I hand it back to those who had it before? Are Plimpton and Rutherford better fitted to wield it than I?

EST. [*Vehemently.*] Give it to the people!

HAGEN. The people! Do you believe that in that mass of ignorance and corruption which you call the people there is the power to rule the world?

EST. What is it that has made the people corrupt? What is it that has kept them in ignorance? What is it but your gold? It lies upon them like a mountain's weight! It crushes every aspiration for freedom . . . every effort after light! Teach them . . . help them . . . then see if they cannot govern themselves!

HAGEN. I meant to do it . . .

EST. Yes . . . so does every rich man! When only he has the time to think of it! When only his power is secure! I have heard my father say it . . . a score of times. But there are always new rivals to trample . . . new foes to fight . . . new wrongs and horrors to be perpetrated! The time to do it is now . . . *now!*

HAGEN. Estelle . . .

CAL. [*Enters hurriedly.*] Prince Hagen!

HAGEN. What is it?

CAL. A message from Isman. There is bad news from Washington.

HAGEN. Well?

CAL. A bill has been introduced in Congress . . . it is expected to pass both houses to-night . . . your property is to be confiscated!

HAGEN. What!

CAL. The sources of natural wealth . . . the land and the mines and the railroads . . . all are to become public property. It is to take effect at once!

EST. [*Pointing at him in exultation.*] Aha! It has come!

They stare at each other.

CAL. I tried to get more information . . . but I was cut off . . .

HAGEN. Cut off!

CAL. I think the wires are down . . . I can't get any response.

HAGEN. I see! [*Stands in deep thought; laughs.*] Well . . . [*To* ESTELLE.] At least Plimpton and Rutherford are buried with me! [*To* CALKINS.] Send to town at once and have the wires seen to. And try to learn what you can.

CAL. Yes, sir . . . at once!

Exit.

EST. They have done it themselves, you see!

HAGEN. Yes . . . I see.

GER. [*Enters, centre; stands looking from one to the other.*] Well, Prince Hagen . . . it looks as if the game was up.

HAGEN. You've heard the news?

GER. From Washington? Yes. And more than that. Your guards have revolted.

HAGEN. What! Here?

GER. Yes. We're prisoners of war, it seems.

EST. Gerald!

HAGEN. How do you know?

GER. They've sent a delegation to tell us. They've

cut the telephone wires, blocked the roads, and shut us in.

HAGEN. What do they want?

GER. They don't condescend to tell us that. They simply inform us that the woods are guarded, and that anyone who tries to leave the camp will be shot.

EST. [*In fright.*] Prince Hagen!

HAGEN *stands motionless.*

GER. [*Solemnly.*] Hagen, the game is up!

HAGEN. [*In deep thought.*] Yes. The game is up. [*A pause.*] Gerald!

GER. Well?

HAGEN. [*Points to violin.*] Play!

GER. [*Startled.*] No!

HAGEN. Play!

GER. You will go?

HAGEN. Yes. I will go. But I will come back! Play! [GERALD *takes the violin and plays the Nibelung theme.*] Louder!

> GERALD *plays the Nibelung music, which is taken up by the orchestra and mounts to a climax, in the midst of which* HAGEN *pronounces a sort of incantation.*

Mimi! Mimi!
Open the gates of wonderland!
Bring back the mood of phantasy, and wake us from our evil dream!

> *Silence. Then answering echoes of the music are heard, faintly, from the fireplace. There are rappings and murmurings underground, rumbling and patter of feet, and all the sounds of Nibelheim. As the music swells louder, the trap doors slide open, and* MIMI *appears, amid steam and glare of light.* ESTELLE *sees him, and recoils in terror. A company of Nibelungs emerge one by one. They peer about*

timidly, recognize HAGEN, *and with much trepidation approach him.* MIMI *clasps his hand, and they surround him with joyful cries. He moves toward the fireplace, and the steam envelops him.*

EST. [*Starts toward him, stretching out her arms to him.*] Prince Hagen!

HAGEN. Farewell!

He gradually retires, and disappears with the Nibelungs. The orchestra sounds the motive of Siegfried Triumphant.

CURTAIN

THE LIBRARY
ST. MARY'S COLLEGE OF MARYLAND
ST. MARY'S CITY, MARYLAND 20686